Mastering
Largemouth
Bass

Mastering Largemouth Bass

Complete Angler's Library ®
North American Fishing Club
Minneapolis, Minnesota

Mastering Largemouth Bass

Copyright © 1989, North American Fishing Club

Library of Congress Catalog Card Number 89-63111
ISBN 0-914697-24-2

Printed in U.S.A.
        12 13 14 15 16 17 18 19

The North American Fishing Club
offers a line of hats for fishermen.
For information, write:
        North American Fishing Club
        P.O. Box 3403
        Minneapolis, MN 55343

Contents

Acknowledgments

Special thanks go to NAFC Publisher Mark LaBarbera, Managing Editor Steve Pennaz, Editorial Assistants Amy Mattson and Amber Weldon, Vice President Product Marketing Mike Vail, Marketing Manager Linda Kalinowski and Art Director Dean Peters. Illustrations by John Buczynski.

Jay Michael Strangis
Managing Editor
Complete Angler's Library

About The Author

In his 35 years of bass fishing, Larry Larsen has literally covered the bass' global range. He has fished as far north as Lake Lida in Minnesota, as far south as Lake Yojoa, Honduras in Central America, as far west as the plantation lakes of the Hawaiian Islands and as far east as Cuba's Treasure Lake.

Larsen has fished bass throughout the Southern and Midwestern states. He has served as a guide for several years on a variety of waters in Florida and Texas, and currently lives on Highland Hills Lake near Lakeland, Florida. He fishes almost daily and has caught and released more than 100 bass exceeding 5 pounds. His personal best largemouth weighed more than 12 pounds. Larsen also established an official line class world record in 1982 for Suwannee bass. His catch has been certified by the National Fresh Water Fishing Hall of Fame.

Larry Larsen has written about bass fishing for more than 20 years. He is the bass columnist for the NAFC's official members-only publication *North American Fisherman* and a frequent contributor to *Outdoor Life*, *Field & Stream*, *Sports Afield* and numerous other national and regional outdoor publications. He has more than 1,000 published articles to his credit. Larsen holds active memberships in the Outdoor Writers

Association of America and the Florida Outdoor Writers Association. He graduated from Wichita State University and attained a master's degree from Colorado State University.

Very few professionals in this country have written more about bass fishing than Larry Larsen. His writings detail highly productive fish-catching methods and special techniques. He believes in giving his readers the latest, most productive tactics to find and catch bass.

Mastering Largemouth Bass will give North American Fishing Club Members a better understanding of North America's number one gamefish—and it will make you a better bass fisherman.

Foreword

Understanding why the largemouth bass is America's number one gamefish is easy. One only has to experience the heart-stopping thrill of hooking one of these battlers to become infatuated with this species. Even more important than its great fighting ability is the largemouth's vast range. In fact, it's a safe bet that most NAFC members live only a short distance from good bass fishing waters.

Largemouth bass are found in every state except Alaska, many of the Canadian provinces, all of the Central American countries and Cuba. Largemouth are also thriving in other areas around the world, including Africa!

Mastering Largemouth Bass was written by Larry Larsen to help NAFC members become better bass fishermen. It takes you step-by-step through the bass fishing process with interesting, easy-to-read text and informative illustrations and photographs.

In Section 1, "Understanding Bass," you'll learn about the bass itself. We'll cover in detail how well a bass can see—information you can use to improve presentations. We'll also explore the bass' sense of smell, which is still not completely understood by some bass fishermen. And we'll discuss the importance of a bass' lateral line and how you can use it to your advantage.

In Section 2, "Where To Find Bass," Larsen tells you how to locate bass, no matter where you are fishing. He talks about ponds and potholes, natural lakes, reservoirs, pits, rivers, swamps—and even brackish tidewater areas! There are tips for eliminating unproductive waters before you start fishing and ways to make topo maps work for you.

Section 3, "How to Catch Bass," describes the most productive ways to fish popular artificials such as crankbaits, plastic worms, jigs and spinnerbaits, as well as tips for fishing shiners, crayfish and other live bait.

Finally, Section 4, "Special Situations," deals with those times when conditions make it difficult to find and catch bass. Larsen takes you through the entire spawning cycle, explaining where to locate the most active fish and techniques to catch them. He also tells you what to do when confronted by severe cold fronts, drastic water level changes and strong winds. NAFC members who can learn how to cope with these conditions will catch fish anytime, anywhere.

Mastering Largemouth Bass will improve your understanding of this fascinating fish and provide a number of fish-catching tips for you to try. But to improve your fishing skill, you must take what you learn here and spend time on the water. Experience is the best teacher. Practice what you learn here and I guarantee you'll catch more bass.

Steve Pennaz
Executive Director
North American Fishing Club

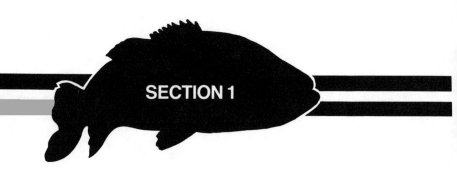

Understanding Bass

1

Sense Of Sight

The butterfly was floating along the canal bulkhead about a foot and a half above the surface. I happened to notice the beautiful golden insect when it flew by an old dock that emerged from a nearby cement-walled shoreline. I stopped casting just long enough to enjoy the sight. Suddenly, the water surface erupted and a 3-pound largemouth shot toward the flapping morsel.

The bass' aim was off so it crashed back into the water without its tasty prey. The event, however, further reinforced my belief that largemouth have very good vision.

The presence of the airborne butterfly was not detected through the bass' sense of smell, sound (lateral line) or taste. The bass saw the butterfly a foot and a half above the canal's surface and reacted quickly. It went for the flying insect and missed.

The accuracy was not a fault of its eyes but more of a miscalculation as to where the moving forage would be as the bass propelled itself skyward. Taking into account the water's refraction of light, the butterfly was a tough target.

A bass' sense of sight is obviously a primary influence on its behavior. Without good vision, bass would have short lifespans. A lot of time and money have been spent to determine just how well largemouth can see, whether they see in color and/or black and white, and whether they see better at night or during the day. NAFC members and tackle companies, as well as fisheries

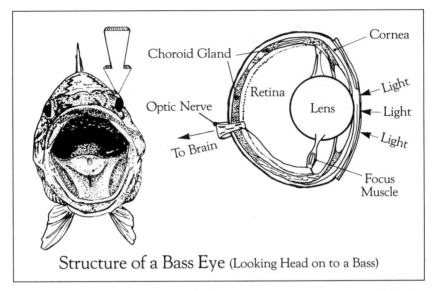

Structure of a Bass Eye (Looking Head on to a Bass)

Labels: Choroid Gland, Retina, Optic Nerve, To Brain, Cornea, Light, Light, Light, Lens, Focus Muscle

Bass eyes have a fixed-focus pupil, which allows them to receive five times more light than human eyes. They do not possess eyelids to protect their eyes.

biologists, have vested interests in uncovering the answers to these questions.

Many facts pertaining to the sight capabilities of the largemouth have recently come to light. Some mysteries of bass vision are yet to be solved; however, knowledge in the area is increasing. For North American Fishing Club members and other anglers, that information translates into better catches.

Eyes play an important part in the day-to-day activities of all predator fish. In most situations and conditions, sight is the dominant sense used in seeking and selecting food.

The largemouth's eyes receive, interpret and respond to light. They also detect movement, form and color. Years of experiments have proven these facts.

The photo sensory cells in a fish's retina consist of cones (for color vision) and rods (for black, white and shades of gray vision). Because of their anatomy, fish's eyes can receive five times more light than the human eye, allowing them to distinguish shapes, sizes, movements and color patterns the human eye can't. And bass can do this under varying water clarity and light conditions!

Bass do not have a nictitating membrane, or eyelid, so they

Fishing may be slow during the first two hours of dark because the largemouth's eye converts to night vision slowly.

Sense Of Sight

can't wink or close their eyes. Instead, their eyes contain a black pigment (not present in human eyes) that shades the photosensitive cells of the retina and allows them to see well in extremely bright conditions with no discomfort.

Although they supposedly have a fixed-focus pupil, bass can and do adjust their eyes to varying light conditions. The lens of the eye moves forward and backward to change the roundness of the eyeball itself, influencing the amount of light entering the eye.

Also, the aquatic environment provides a tremendous filter that allows the largemouth to be comfortable in the bright, high-noon sun. In fact, larger bass spend more time in brightly lit areas than do juveniles. They have less to fear than smaller specimens.

NAFC members often catch lunkers during the mid-day sun periods. Some experienced big-bass guides even claim that they catch the majority of 10-pound-plus fish then. My own experience on waters less than 10 feet deep has proven that the percentage of large bass strikes increases between 10 a.m. and 2 p.m.

Even though bass can spend a great deal of time in the sun without eye protection, they will often use a shady spot for ambushing their prey. In fact, a feeding bass will do just that. The visual acuity of the largemouth increases about three-fold when looking into sunlit areas from shady ones.

Forage moving about in the sunlight have difficulty seeing the predator in the shade, but the reverse is not true. The wise bass positions itself to take advantage of this vision superiority. And it normally succeeds.

Bass have an extremely wide field of vision, a full 180 degrees for each eye. That allows them binocular vision in front and slightly upward due to the overlap of field. They see objects mirrored on the water such as the butterfly, which it views as proportionally larger when directly overhead.

The eyes of the largemouth are positioned for good side (although monocular) vision, but the fish are most effective at striking prey and lures in their binocular zone. "Blind" areas exist to the rear and under the bass.

Research shows that a largemouth's vision improves with its age. A bass' eyes continue to grow throughout its life regardless

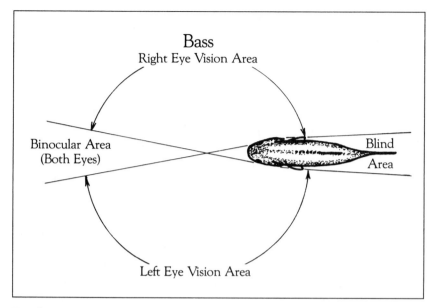

Bass have a forward eye position, which increases their binocular vision and enhances coordination when striking at prey.

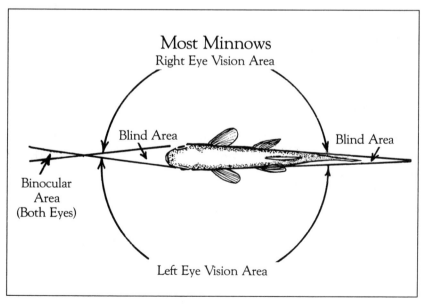

Most prey fish have eyes located laterally, which reduces their binocular vision but enables them to view in all directions.

of body growth. Maybe that's another reason that lunkers are difficult to fool with artificial lures.

Can large bass distinguish real and fake forage more easily than smaller ones? All I know is that winning the lunker bass game requires careful planning and attention to detail. Timing, bait selection and presentation are usually the key elements in successfully catching a big largemouth.

The bass' eyes are programmed for both day and nighttime vision. During the daylight hours, the sensitive cones in the retina move forward and the rods move backward. At night the movement is reversed and they use their black-and-white cone vision system.

Periods when light levels change, such as dusk and dawn, are interesting. Our eyes adjust to the change much more quickly than those of a bass—about 30 minutes for most humans. Bass and other fish aren't so fortunate. At dusk, the rods in the bass' eye migrate forward in the retina for after-dark vision.

It takes almost two hours for the largemouth's eye to become programmed for night vision. Then, at about two hours before first light, the transition back to the daylight mode begins. Thus, contrary to what most anglers have been taught, fishing may be extremely slow the first two hours of dark and during the last two before daylight.

Daylight or color vision is vital to the life of the largemouth. Most bass rely on their color vision for foraging, self-defense and for mating signals. Tests show that bass have excellent color vision and can readily distinguish between narrow (closely related) color bands. According to research studies, they can also discriminate between different shades of the same color.

Knowing how certain parameters of water and light characteristics affect bass vision and bait selection enables anglers to have a better shot at aggressive feeders. But until recently, very little had been proven about color preferences of bass.

Over the years, most anglers' best guesses have been based on individual experiences. The lures we've selected have been the lures that worked on similar days in the past. We've based the color choice on such factors as cloud cover, water clarity,

The color preference of bass depends on their environment and the time of day. Selecting the right color combinations for your lure can pay large dividends.

angle of the sun and water depth. Often, the chosen weapon worked and we caught numerous bass on a specific lure. But just as often our educated guesses were wrong.

Findings by Dr. Loren Hill, chairman of the University of Oklahoma's Zoology Department and Director of Biological Research, confirm and refute many anglers' field observations. His nine-year study of bass vision and the color sensitivity of largemouth at given water visibilities and light has resulted in many interesting, but controversial, theories.

Dr. Hill tested color discrimination, sensitivity and preference in bass. In a nutshell, his results showed that bass were sensitive to all colors tested, and they could even discriminate between green, blue green, light green and dark green.

Additional testing was designed to determine the degree of color sensitivity of the bass to a variety of different colors, including both fluorescent and nonfluorescent. Results after several days of tests indicated that bass do not respond equally to different colors with the same stimuli. The bass' responses to colors, while varying the water clarity, time and sky parameters, revealed that color selections were unique to a particular environmental condition.

During each experiment, the exact light transmittance value was recorded by means of a light meter, reading 0 to 100 percent. These values, recorded for water clarity, time of day and sky condition, were then duplicated to the exact percentile value for the colored food preference experiments.

The end result of Dr. Hill's extensive testing was the Color-C-Lector, which is now being marketed by Lake Systems Division of Mount Vernon, Missouri.

The instrument is easy to use. By dropping the probe into the water at any depth, the light transmittance value is correlated to the color most visible to the bass under that particular water clarity, time of day and sky condition. For example, if the lure you plan to use runs five feet deep, simply lower the probe to that depth and the Color-C-Lector will tell you what color should be the most productive.

"By observing the colors adjacent to the color indicated on the band, anglers can even select the right color combo," says Dr. Hill. "The instrument will reliably predict the combination that will yield the greatest percentage of strikes!"

The largemouth's eyes take a couple of hours to adjust from daylight to night vision, so during that period, a light background behind the prey enables them to have a better view of prey in the foreground.

Many prominent anglers and fisheries biologists dispute Dr. Hill's conclusions. All concur that color makes a tremendous difference in fishing success, but they have difficulty believing that fish strike the color they can see best at a certain time.

Some also contend they experienced problems with the calibrations; different units gave different readings when used side by side under similar light conditions. Still, many anglers swear by the Color-C-Lector.

"The thing to remember is the color arrangement is not what one would expect," Dr. Hill admits. "We expect long wavelengths (red and orange) to physically filter out with water depth, whereas the short wavelengths (blues and greens) should penetrate deeper."

"However, in waters with suspended particles such as silt, clay debris and various forms of plankton, light is absorbed, scattered, reflected and/or refracted," says Dr. Hill. "Bottom color such as white sand may cause the lower layer of water to have more light than mid-layers."

Thus, the physics of color wavelength penetration are not relevant as to what colors bass can see. Red may not become black to a bass at 20 feet. In other words, don't select lure colors based on the predictable principle of red light not being visible in deep, muddy water. You may not be fishing with the most visible colors.

Another point for NAFC members to remember is that color in any lure depends on the light reflected off the object. Thus, color at the surface could be perceived very differently 15 feet down.

Why the emphasis on color preferences of bass? Most forage fish take on different colors at different stages of life and under various environmental conditions. Scale tints and fins of certain species change during the mating season, for example.

While we can learn some behavioral characteristics through observation and experimentation, we will never know just exactly what bass see. They perceive color differently than we do. In my many hours of scuba diving, I have yet to view that environment through the eyes of a largemouth. No one has.

2

Sense Of Smell

Most kids who grew up in the Midwest used the foulest-smelling concoctions they could find to catch catfish. I was no exception. I would leave a jar of chicken entrails in the sun for a few days, knowing that the worse it smelled, the better the catfish would like it. And believe it or not, I caught fish.

Back then, though, few knew that the black bass even had a nose, let alone used it. Only recently has any attention been given to the bass' sense of smell. How good is it? Research biologists are still testing, but the tackle industry has introduced a boatload of effective bass scents. And bass fishermen are buying them.

Annual scent sales are in the neighborhood of $40 to $50 million. More than 50 manufacturers are marketing scent products. Berkley, Johnson Fishing, Normark and other manufacturers have jumped into the lucrative market. Each has numerous testimonials from fisheries biologists, weekend fishermen and professional anglers who swear these products help them catch more bass.

While a great deal of research has been conducted on the olfactory systems (sense of smell) of salmon and catfish, comparatively little has been done on bass. We do know that a bass' sense of smell is not as keen as that of a salmon or catfish, but it is much better than previously thought, according to Berkley fish researcher Dr. Keith Jones. He notes that bass

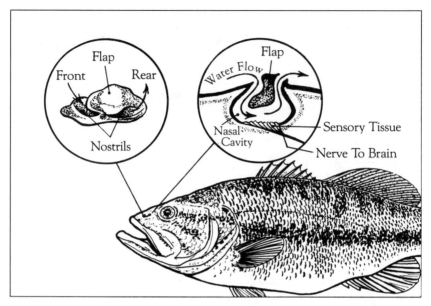

A bass has an excellent sense of smell. Water passes through its nose and stimulates sensory tissue that sends signals to its brain.

discriminate scent much better than even the best bird dog.

How Bass Use Their Noses

Any discussion of bass' sense of smell should consider how they use it, i.e., for foraging or protection, and when. Bass utilize their full range of senses especially when visibility is limited. Smell becomes increasingly important in low light situations.

Biologists note that bass communicate with one another through "chemical communication." They can even recognize their own kind by a particular smell. Each fish has a distinctive body odor. Tests show that some laboratory minnow specimens can be trained to distinguish the odors of more than a dozen different species of fish.

The smell of a predator fish alarms forage fish, sometimes triggering them to flee. Some forage species release an alarm substance when danger threatens. Injured baitfish have a traumatic effect on the remainder of the school. They seemingly cause the school to reel in fright. Although release of such an alarm substance hasn't been proven as a bass attractant, they may very well be able to detect it.

Bass preyfish are composed of amino acids, the building blocks of all protein and flesh. Each species contains differing proportions of amino acids. The injury of a preyfish and release of amino acids elicits a searching behavior from the bass. A scent product with the right combination of amino acids could be attractive to bass.

Tests by bass researcher Dr. Loren Hill show that bass can detect a preyfish odor source at a distance of 25 feet. Only the bass' sense of hearing is capable of greater range under normal water clarity conditions. Hill points out that the bass exhibit a snakelike swimming action when honing in on an odor source.

Bass' scenting powers also enable them to find their way back to certain feeding flats. Tests with displaced bass show that most can return to their home territory by utilizing their olfactory perception, much like salmon returning to their streams of birth.

Bass also use their sense of smell to distinguish between types of weeds. Each kind of aquatic plant has a characteristic smell, and bass may prefer one over another because of odor preferences. Fish also use their olfactory powers in their territorial claims. The dominance of larger bass over smaller ones may be based on the odors given off and received.

The sense of smell also plays a role in reproduction. Bass return to certain spawning areas year after year because of smell. Also, females produce a chemical in their ovaries that causes males to exhibit courtship behavior. We can conclude that the sense of smell has a bearing on bass' entire social behavior.

The Olfactory System Of The Bass

A bass has a pair of nostrils, or nares, on each side of its head between the eye and upper lip. Each nostril has two openings separated by a bridge of skin. Water circulates continuously through these short passageways where microscopic, hair-like cilia detect odors. The water is then expelled without entering the throat.

As a bass swims about, water movement is enhanced and the nostrils are constantly in use. A membrane tissue, called the olfactory epithelium, consists of complex folds that line the nostrils. This membrane greatly increases the total surface area

Scent products are not only employed to attract bass but also to mask human smell and other potential turnoffs. A drop or two is all it takes.

and the bass' receptive scenting powers.

Within the epithelium odor molecules activate several million olfactory receptor nerve cells. These send a message to the olfactory centers of the brain, where the odor is interpreted.

Many bass researchers believe in the "lock and key" receptor theory. It proposes that specific molecular depressions (locks) exist on the surfaces of the receptor cells and only a particular odor molecule (key) can fit. The depression sensors, called chemoreceptors, respond only to those odorant molecules that have the appropriate chemical shape to fit.

Chemoreception, according to many scientists, is the most primitive sense in the universe. Bass use this to avoid harmful pH conditions, to flee from harmful chemicals, and to find food and suitable dissolved oxygen content. Many believe it rules the bass' entire behavior.

Aging And Size Factors

As bass grow older and larger, the number of olfactory folds increases. Dr. Mike Howell, head of Samford University's Biology Department, found that young, 4- to 6-inch largemouth

Bass use their full range of senses. When the visibility is limited, smell becomes extremely important in relation to the closing distance from an object.

Sense Of Smell

bass have five or six olfactory folds. A 12-inch bass may have 10 folds while one measuring 20 inches could have nearly 20 folds. Dr. Howell also found that the diameter of the olfactory organ itself increases with age. Most scientists conclude that older bass have a better developed sense of smell. Mature fish exhibit some behavioral characteristics that fingerlings don't, such as claiming territories and spawning. They use their better developed olfactory powers for those actions.

Scent Products Everywhere

Scents have been used for years in both salt- and freshwater. Chum and natural bait-tipped jigs have always worked to entice fish. Many NAFC members know the affection catfish have for a variety of doughbaits and other smelly elixirs. Plastic worms have been pouched in aromatic oils for years. Pork rind and the salt-impregnated rubber products introduced a few years back have certainly caught more than their share of fish. Why? Because they appeal to the bass' olfactory powers.

The rage for adding secret "potions" to a lure or bait is over, but thousands of anglers still use scents religiously. The scent's ability to attract bass is paramount to its success. Scent molecules sometimes permeate water slowly, yet they can be carried off quickly by current.

Some anglers report negative effects from using a scent product, but complaints are few. Most users find the response of bass to be either positive (they strike the lure or bait) or neutral (no discernible effect on the catch rate).

Certainly there are times when bass will hit a bait whether it has scent on it or not, and there are times when they won't hit a bait even when it is coated with scent. Most anglers hope the scent will convince the "iffy" fish to take the bait. The scent, they hope, makes their artificial lure or bait more appealing or natural to the predator bass.

Not all scent products are designed to attract fish. Many of them are designed to mask human smell and other potential turnoffs. Their use camouflages any smell transferred to the lure or bait from handling or other means. In order to be most productive, experts tell us odors from gasoline, insect repellent, reel oil and human sweat should be masked.

A few products give off tiny oil bubbles as they disperse.

Others dissolve slowly and are said to last longer. The time between applications depends on which product you are using and to whom you are talking. The array of scents on the market today last anywhere from five casts to 30 minutes.

You can use too much of a good thing, however. A good example is someone who wears too much of a powerful perfume or cologne. The same thing is true with fish scents. You can overpower the olfactory system by saturating the water with scent. A dab or two in the right places is attractive, a splash here and a splash there is a turnoff.

Manufacturers based their scent formulas on several premises. One is centered on the amino acid composition of various forage species. There are 20 basic amino acids that serve as protein building blocks. Some of these amino acids attract fish, while others repel them.

The fish attractants based on particular combinations of amino acids claim they have the correct profile for various forage species like crayfish and shad. The thought is that a bass feeding primarily on shad can distinguish distinctive shad odor from other water-based odors.

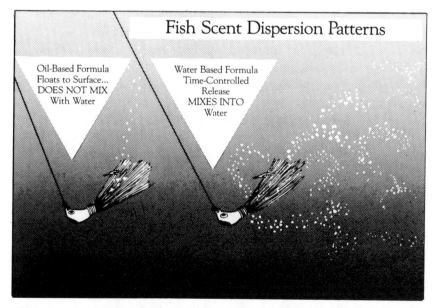

Fish Scent Dispersion Patterns

Oil-Based Formula
Floats to Surface...
DOES NOT MIX
With Water

Water Based Formula
Time-Controlled
Release
MIXES INTO
Water

Many bass researchers believe that attractants must dissolve into the water in a time-controlled manner to be effective. Water-soluble fish scents disperse around the lure.

Other concepts of scent formulation include pheromones and aromatic (non-pheromone or amino acid) odors. Pheromones are chemical messengers that influence behavior in the same species. Examples include fear and reproductive chemicals, which might have some interesting possibilities if introduced into a scent product. Fear pheromones from a shad and sex pheromones from a female bass might cause a male bass to be aggressive.

Anise oil is a longtime additive to plastic lures and an excellent example of an aromatic odor. Other aromatics, such as food product aromas, have been added to various lures over the years. The addition of a grape jelly flavor has been more commonly thought of as a scent mask rather than an attractant.

A variety of scent products line the shelves of most tackle shops. Some are the result of research and development from amino acids. Others are extracts from natural forage. Still others contain fear and sex pheromones.

For soft baits, many liquids do the job. They adhere better than solids to plastic worms, jigs, spinnerbait skirts and pork. Solid attractants can be molded to precede a lure, as can a piece of foam rubber soaked in a liquid attractant. Scent products generally don't last long when applied to slick finishes.

Optimal conditions for use of a scent product may be in cold water when bass rely more on their sense of smell, after cold fronts when bass are not aggressively chasing lures, and when fishing slow-moving lures. Then again, the best time could simply be whenever you have a chance to use the product. Regardless of when you decide to apply some fish attractant, it's quite possible that you may catch larger fish that appear to have a more well-developed olfactory system.

Scent manufacturers claim that their products work on inactive bass. Obviously, an active fish will hit just about anything. The difference between consistently catching large numbers of bass or a few is in attracting the inactive fish. Utilizing scents on your lures or baits is an option you may want to experiment with. Above all, you should fish scented lures slower than you normally fish. Bass apparently take their time analyzing the smell of a lure or bait. An inactive fish, given time to discern the scent, may decide to feed on the lure or bait. The scent may trigger the bass' striking mechanism.

Larger bass like this one held by the author rely heavily on their olfactory system when feeding. The use of scent may make your offerings more appealing to these fish.

Of course, NAFC members must remember that bass utilize all of their senses. The degree to which they depend on each varies with conditions. When sight and scent are reduced, hearing can become most vital.

3

Sense Of Hearing

The black bass is an uncanny predator. It can explode on a floating plug in dark, muddy water. It can easily capture forage fish after dark, and seek and destroy bait in heavy cover. How does it pinpoint such objects when it can't rely solely on its eyes or sense of smell? Quite easily.

Bass utilize their full range of senses, especially hearing, when visibility is limited. Sound helps bass find forage in waters of marginal clarity. Hearing is the bass' most acute sense, but it is largely misunderstood. Bass detect sound through their lateral line at a distance of up to 100 feet—about twice as far as they can see!

Humans normally rely first on their sense of sight and then on their sense of hearing for interpretation. The order while eating is normally sight, smell and then taste. Bass, on the other hand, frequently rely first on their sense of sound while foraging or to detect possible harm. Sound and vibration travel four times faster in water than they do in air.

In water, sound waves are transmitted directly at 5,000 feet per second with very little "buffering" or loss of magnitude. Thus, the signal strength of a rattling bait, such as a Norman Little "N" as it is cranked through turbid water will be easily detected by bass in the vicinity. The sound coming off the moving, rattling lure will be more discernible to a bass below the surface than to a human above.

How Bass Hear

The idea that bass are able to detect sound and process the stimuli has evolved over the years. Today, fisheries biologists are sure that bass have excellent hearing and that they are sensitive to all sounds in their environment.

Bass have a complete auditory system. The basic biological difference between a fish's hearing system and ours is the fish's lack of a cochlea, or pitch discriminator. They use other means to discriminate pitch.

Bass detect distant sounds with their inner ear. They identify closer sounds through their lateral line. At distances of more than 20 feet, a bass will hear the sound with its inner ear, a complex structure of interlocking rings located within the skull. Sounds, particularly those of high frequencies, are transmitted through the skin, muscle and bone to the inner ear, but the bass will not be able to detect the source or its location.

To pinpoint objects, bass utilize their lateral line, which is a series of sensitive nerve endings that extend from just behind the gills to the tail on each side of the fish. The lateral line is a displacement-pressure receptor that "feels" the pressure waves created by objects moving through the water. The line is sensitive to the low frequency sounds that are more commonly transmitted underwater. While in a fast-moving school, bass use their lateral lines to avoid colliding with each other.

At distances less than 20 feet, bass employ their lateral line to detect underwater vibrations and noise sources. When alerted to such disturbances, fish become wary with their fins erect. They often form a circle facing outward, according to fisheries biologist Dr. Loren Hill.

"The sound/distance factor is significant if you are wading, tube fishing or fishing from a boat in an area with very little cover," he says. "So, when casting in waters with sparse cover, attempt to throw long distances. To accomplish this, position your boat more than 20 feet away from the target."

The underwater world is not as silent as some anglers think. Hydrophone placement by acoustic experts reveals that many creatures in the aquatic environment make sounds. Drum, for example, make a resonating noise by flexing muscles attached to the walls of their swim bladders.

Bass are very aware of the sounds that are normal parts of

The sound of a lure moving on the water's surface will be more discernible to a bass below than to the angler above.

their environment. Some fish use sound in their mating rituals or as warning signals to aggressors. Crayfish and freshwater shrimp make clicking sounds, according to acoustics experts. Large crayfish often emit claw-snapping and antenna-scraping sounds. Also, initial underwater contact between predator and prey is not usually by sight or smell but through sound waves.

Bass themselves sound off by flaring and closing their gill covers. A largemouth protecting its territory or spawning bed will spread its fins and open and close its gills with a resounding clap to scare away intruders. I've often seen this behavior while scuba diving near male bass protecting their beds. At times I could even hear them slamming their gills shut. It's mighty intimidating, believe me!

Vibrating baits are easily picked up by bass through their lateral line. These baits are very effective in muddy water but produce well in clear water, too!

Motivating Forces

Sound may or may not motivate a response from bass. It depends on several factors, such as the type of sound, depth of water, water clarity and how accustomed the bass are to a particular sound. Loud, sharp noises in a boat, like dropping a tackle box or anchor, can spook bass.

Boat traffic will often turn off a school of feeding bass, but not always. Sometimes bass will not pay attention to any passing craft. Deep-water largemouth, especially those in waters more than 15 feet deep, are generally undisturbed by the sound of a nearby outboard motor.

Shallow-water bass show an awareness of engine noise but react little to the disturbance. That is not true, however, if you roar up to a school of feeding bass and shut off the engine. You will, more than likely, spook these fish.

A better approach is to idle slowly up to the activity and shut off the motor. Then bass will continue their feeding, allowing you to get in on some fast action. In lakes with high boat traffic, like those near major metropolitan areas, bass are usually accustomed to the sounds of racing outboards.

There are times, believe it or not, when boat traffic can stimulate bass feeding activity. Boats moving down rivers and smaller tributaries often create a wake, which disturbs shoreline sanctuaries. This dislodges and scatters crayfish, minnows and other forage into vulnerable areas. Bass then associate the sounds of boat engines with the veritable feast.

I've often been anchored over a drop-off in a river and noticed that whenever another boat would pass, I would soon get a strike. The noisy boat did not destroy my fishing but enhanced it.

Another trick that many NAFC members have used successfully is trolling along the banks of a river or lake. Bass are sometimes attracted to shoreline by the vibrations and feed actively.

Many anglers know that sounds can attract. They take their extra-long poles and vigorously thrash the water in low-light or no-light situations. The noise often attracts bass because they think the commotion was caused by feeding fish and they want to join in the feast. Twitching an injured minnow or topwater plug in the area often leads to explosive strikes, especially in muddy water.

Bass attribute many types of water disturbance to a feeding opportunity. Early Native Americans reportedly attracted fish to their nets and snares by clacking two rocks together underwater. There is little evidence that fish are as affected by sounds made above water. Though researchers have proven that a fish's hearing is acute enough to distinguish noise and tone above water, normal tones of voice do not generate a significant response from bass.

Noisy Lure Choices

Some lures rely on sound for their effectiveness. Lure manufacturers create more productive baits with the knowledge that bass can hear. Many experiment with lure designs that emit sounds at frequencies that attract bass.

Trying to duplicate the sounds of forage, lure makers place shot in the chambers of moving plugs. Many companies insert rattles in most of their hard baits, such as crankbaits, topwater plugs and vibrating lures. Rattles are now being implanted into spinnerbaits, jig heads and even soft plastic lures.

Lures that make noise sell well and catch bass. It's easy to hear a good rattling crankbait moving through the water if you are scuba diving. When diving, I've heard plugs from more than 20 feet away. Boat anglers sometimes hear crankbaits as they are cranked near the boat.

Topwater lures are generally noisy. They often pop, slash or churn up the surface, begging for attention. Other baits, such as plastic worms or rubber plugs, send off a natural "plop" as they land. That attracts the attention of bass. Don't believe that a worm crawling along the bottom doesn't send off significant sound waves. It does.

Soft, nonthreatening noises are the best to use in relatively shallow, calm environments. When the wind is howling, however, it may take some effort to get a bass' attention. Likewise, in muddy water the "squeaking wheel" may get the attention from a bass. The noisemakers in such conditions are simply more effective.

There are several other rules to remember about sound when fishing. Loud, unfamiliar sounds spook bass, while most lures either attract or have a neutral effect on the fish. Throwing out your anchor literally alerts every fish for a hundred yards to your presence, and intruders in the underwater world are not welcome.

Boat noise in general spooks bass and should be kept to a minimum. Carpet the bottom of your boat if tackle box clanging or other noises are common. Don't use a metal stringer if fishing from an aluminum boat. Prevention is the hallmark of a quiet, productive angler.

Electric motors sometimes scare fish. Noisy ones that are constantly turned on and off are the worst culprits. I own a super-quiet Evinrude Scout that I try to run on a low speed to minimize disturbance. I've run the bow of my bass boat up into rushes and caught bass beside the boat within five seconds of turning off the electric, even in extremely shallow water.

Crankbaits with rattles often emit a "clicking" sound that some say mimics the noises of a shad school. The vibrations of deep-running cranks seem to draw plenty of strikes.

Sense Of Hearing

45

In muddy water, bass depend on their ability to transmit the action of the lure they are tracking to the brain for interpretation. At night, or on waters of medium to low visibility, sound and vibration play a vital role in an NAFC member's success.

Most diving and many topwater lures are constructed with either rattling devices or spinners to attract the attention of bass. Sound often plays a key role in drawing the strike. The bass' lateral line translates messages from the external world through nerve impulses to the brain. To the predator, the message is often "follow and kill."

Through sight, scent and sound we have seen how largemouth bass operate. With exceptional sensory powers, how do record bass fall prey to man's imitations? It's due to a need they share with us...the need to eat.

=4=

Bass Feeding Behavior

The largemouth bass has one major weakness—its never-ending quest for food. Its insatiable appetite is one reason anglers pursue this highly popular freshwater gamefish. A bass grows fast and grows large because it is constantly foraging. This habit makes the bass susceptible to anglers.

While a baby bass' mouth is developing during the first few hours after it emerges tail-first from the egg, the yolk sac sustains it. The bass' eyes are bigger than its stomach from about the second or third day of life. By this time, the yolk sac has been absorbed and the fingerling is ready for the world. From then on, the bass continuously searches for forage to satisfy its basic energy needs.

Since smaller bass require less food for maintenance, a greater percentage of the forage eaten is utilized for growth. As its size increases, the food intake as a percentage of body weight decreases. The bass eats voraciously and continues to grow.

The size of prey consumed by a largemouth increases as the fish grows, though the relative size decreases. The types of forage utilized also changes. A transition in food habits occurs. Baby bass feast on plant and animal microorganisms at first. The principal food for bass less than 2 inches is plankton and tiny crustaceans (zooplankton and water fleas). These small bass seem to feed endlessly. After four to six weeks, aquatic and terrestrial insects, especially nymph and larvae forms, become

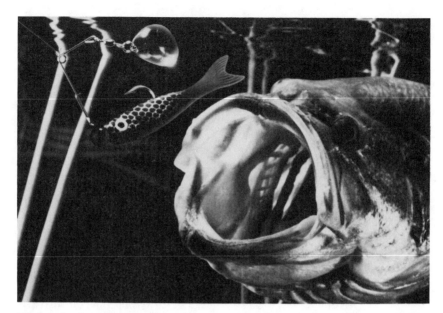

The bass has one major weakness—its never-ending quest for food. NAFC members who understand the bass' feeding process will catch more fish.

important ingredients in the bass' diet until it is about 4 inches long. A small bass ingests amazing numbers of mosquito larvae at this time.

At about 10 weeks, the diet of a fingerling bass consists mostly of tiny forage fish and other small, edible creatures such as crayfish and grass shrimp. They are soon feeding on anything they can get into their mouths, including their smaller siblings. Within six months they have usually attained a length of 6 or 7 inches and are not particular about what they eat. Forage fish, frogs and large crustaceans become even more substantial parts of their diet when they reach a pound or more in size.

Fearsome Bass

When a bass reaches 2 to 5 pounds, it has matured into an efficient predator. It gains the respect of all forage that is proportionately smaller. Besides smaller forage fish, the bass' diet may consist of ducklings, water snakes, field mice, baby alligators, birds or any small insect that falls into the water. This predator is feared by those in its aquatic environment and should be feared by some on land.

I have seen some large bass tackle very big forage fish. I once found an 8-pounder floating dead with a 2-pound bream stuck in its mouth. A largemouth can supposedly swallow a slab-sided bluegill that is about one-third its own length. Keeping this in mind when you go to the tackle box could pay big dividends.

The feeding habits of the largemouth bass are influenced by the following: degree of hunger, maturity and size of fish, sex of fish, spawning activities, water temperature, time of day and year, and the many forage factors. Forage factors to consider include: size distribution, coloration, mobility, accessibility, abundance of primary forage and alternative food supplies, length of growing season, amount of cover, amount of fishing pressure, abundance of other predators, turbidity and productivity of the water and armament, such as spines or shells.

Digestive Influence

Digestive rates vary with several parameters that are keyed to the bass' metabolism. Bass strike baits or lures even with a full stomach. Many of us have caught bass that were spitting up food and yet still trying to swallow our baits.

Water temperature affects the metabolism of the cold-blooded fish. As winter sets in, dropping temperatures into the 40s, the bass' metabolism rate and correspondingly, its digestion rate, slow down. Food requirements also reduce at lower temperatures. Feeding activity is influenced less by the hunger factor since bass feed as infrequently as once every two weeks in extremely cold water.

The bass' digestive physiology limits the type of food it utilizes. Enzymes that break down protein and fat are present in its stomach and intestines, but those digestive enzymes required for breakdown of vegetation are not. A check of the stomach contents of any bass cleaned should reveal food in various stages of digestion. It takes about two days for a bass to completely digest most forage fish during warm weather and longer in cold temperatures.

Feeding Motivation

You will commonly find three types of feeding behavior in lake and stream bass. They are methodical inhalation,

Bass traveling in schools often herd threadfin shad to the surface. The baitfish are most vulnerable when their movements are limited. Low light levels due to clouds enhance the effectiveness of such open-water attacks.

competitive inspiration and reflex reaction. While the first two behaviors are hunger-driven, the latter is simply a response to the newly found prey.

A solitary bass spots its victim from either an ambush or cruising position. It approaches the prey with caution and opens its huge mouth to inhale the food. The mouth opening sucks in whatever happens to be near it. The gills flare simultaneously with the mouth's opening to discharge the adjacent water through the gill covers, thus creating suction through its mouth. The action is quick and the predator doesn't even have to be right on target.

The bass, upon recognizing a phony forage, quickly reverses the action and blows it out. The suction, while deadly to prey, is often hard to detect from the surface side of a fishing rig. Line stretch and rod vibration make it difficult for anglers to determine what is happening on the end of their monofilament and to decide if the bait has just been exhaled or if it's time to set the hook. NAFC members must utilize careful observation and a sensitive rod to detect this type of strike action by a bass.

Eternal Competition

Bass always compete with each other for available forage. This is especially true in years of low forage population due to poor forage spawning production. For bass, less food per acre means an unbalanced fishery and survival of the fittest.

When competing with others in the area for the same food, bass charge the forage and quickly engulf it. When an angler's lure fools a bass, other bass compete for that bait. A similar lure tossed near the action by a second NAFC member often brings a strike from a competing member of the bass school. Trailing bass get excited about losing the forage and attack the second lure.

Likewise, when a surfacing fish pops a frog or bream, the angler who gets the lure to that spot quickly often connects with the feeding bass or one of its competitors. These fish have very little thought of safety when they are on a feeding binge. Even when a bass is full, it may want to beat the competition to a newly introduced prey. It can't stand another fish beating it out of the food.

Bass normally school according to year class, but the size range may vary. A four-year-old largemouth can weigh 8 pounds or 1, depending on how competitive it is. A school of fish spawned in a particular year often stays together until the population dwindles substantially. The size of a bass school may vary from six fish to more than 400, depending on the structure present and forage available. The weight of the bass may vary by 100 percent. Four-pounders may coexist with 2-pounders, creating stiff competition.

Hunger Ritual

When hunger motivates feeding bass, they exhibit a unique behavior that includes preparatory movements. When forage fish notice the activity, which includes a rocking motion of the bass' body and the flaring of its gills, they frantically seek cover. Until the hunger urge and corresponding antics occur, the underwater world appears calm and serene.

On numerous occasions, underwater researchers and observers have watched bass and other predators swim among their forage, passing within inches of them. The potential food is unconcerned about the nearby predator and shows little

A large bass prefers large forage. Keep that in mind when fishing trophy fish.

caution. Shiners, bluegill and other forage are not frightened by the presence of even huge bass. The obvious compatibility of predator and prey adds to the tranquility and peacefulness of the aquatic scene.

Carl Malz, a well-known magazine editor, describes the underwater ritual he observed on a bass fishing trip in Rainbow Springs, Florida.

"Suddenly, the entire mood and tempo of the scene began to change," he said. "Both the shad and the bluegill began to fidget nervously. Smaller baitfish darted restlessly from place to place. Other schools of roving baitfish deserted their open-water positions in favor of stations located much closer to weed or brush-type cover.

"While all this nervous activity was going on amongst the forage fish, one huge bass began to display a rhythmic flexing of its jaws. It flared its gills several times, raised its dorsal fin and its eyes began to move in rapid, jerky motions.

"I noticed the bass also changed to a vivid green," Carl continued. "Even the black stripe along its lateral line turned darker and was far more distinguishable.

"Then an entire school of very large bass, some in the 9- or 10-pound range, slowly emerged from a bunch of weeds. When they reached the outer edge of the weedline they stopped for a second and started yawning and flaring their gill covers like the first bass. Their eyeballs also started to dart back and forth, and all raised their dorsal fins.

"You should have seen the baitfish then," he said. "The bluegill, shad and baitfish population went absolutely bananas. They scattered in every direction. But it didn't help much. That school of lunker bass charged from the weedline and tore into them as if there were no tomorrow. If you can visualize a hungry pack of wolves intimidating its prey, then you have a clear picture of what was happening down there."

Such behavior usually lasts only minutes. The aggressive prowlers select their prey and quickly catch them. Then, as suddenly as the mood changed, the scene reverts back to calmness. The frenzy is over. The baitfish no longer dart into heavy vegetation. They emerge from hiding. The bass' danger signals cease and the prey is safe to swim out in the open again, at least for the time being.

Bass prefer to attack prey they can catch off guard rather than chase forage in open water.

Quick Reaction

The third type of feeding behavior exhibited by bass is the reflex response. This reaction is usually not inspired by hunger. Many of the strikes that anglers get are of this nature. The angler's lure splashing down near the fish may key the instantaneous response. You see the same behavior when you toss a minnow into a large tank with bass. The nearest bass immediately hits it.

Often the predators are full at the time of such behavior. A properly presented lure or bait triggers the reflex action. It's simply an instinctive reaction by the bass to what it believes to be forage moving near it. The retrieval speed of an artificial bait that garners this response depends, in part, on water temperature. Warmer weather brings on quicker actions, and faster retrieves give you better catches of bass.

You can also trick feeding bass into this response. Those on the prowl looking for something to eat will pounce on baits as they hit the water. Therefore, keeping a keen eye out for any sign of feeding enables an angler to trigger a reflex strike more often.

Fill It Up

NAFC members find feeding bass in shallow or deep waters. Targets holding forage can be located easily in the shallows. Search deeper waters with depthfinders to discover areas with good cover. Bass normally spread out over a shallow area as they hunt for food, but they remain schooled on a particular spot while foraging the depths.

Bass quickly fill up when the prey is abundant, easily caught and of substantial size. If forage is small or hard to catch the bass feed for longer periods. They burn energy more quickly during such marathon feeding periods and require even more energy. It is a continuous process, a closed cycle. Bass burn energy rapidly while chasing smaller forage.

As the forage base grows or better feeding conditions are discovered elsewhere, they expend less energy to fill the stomach. Bass then require shorter feeding times.

In cold water, bass feed less and less. Unless a bass finds warm water during extreme winter periods, its urge to feed diminishes substantially.

Forage Abstinence

A fish's sex plays a part in its feeding habits. The good news for NAFC members is that larger female bass feed more actively than males. But there are times when male bass are more susceptible to capture, especially during the spawn when they are guarding the nest, even though they seldom feed during this part of the spring.

While the males build the nests, they will try to keep invaders away from the area. They are very protective against any potential egg-eating predator, such as bluegill, salamanders, crayfish and certain minnow species. A lure crawled through a bed at this time triggers the protective reaction, a non-feeding response.

Meanwhile, the females lie in nearby deep water showing no interest in feeding. Baitfish move freely among the ripe sows knowing full-well they are safe. Female bass that do feed while on the bed often take what appears to be injured forage. They won't expend much energy chasing anything. They'll simply suck in a bait gently to check out its edibility.

After spawning, the big females are physically spent. Their

energy is drained and forage is difficult for them to catch. Tempting baitfish swim among the lethargic bass without fear for a few weeks until the females regain full strength. The easiest prey at this time is often their own young.

The young bass quickly learn that their own parents will eat them. Most large females are cannibalistic and smaller bass must stay constantly alert to survive. Some very large bass (up to 4 pounds) have been found in the throats and stomachs of trophy largemouth!

Depth Behavior

The presence of other predators influences the relationship between bass and their prey. In lakes where northern pike and walleye compete with bass for young perch, some studies show that bass modify their foraging. The abundance of northerns, in particular, influences the depth zones and type of structure bass use, according to biologists with the Minnesota Department of Natural Resources.

Water level greatly influences how and when bass eat. When water levels are up and into dense aquatic vegetation, bass tend to feed heavily on crayfish, which are usually abundant in the weedy shallows. As the water recedes and vegetation declines, bass consumption of crayfish decreases, and consumption of shad and bluegill increases. Bass' consumption of crayfish is relative to the amount of vegetation a body of water contains.

Lake managers who wish to control the predator-prey relationship in their waters usually do so through water level fluctuation. This occurs naturally or through droughts and floods due to irrigation, runoffs and drawdowns. Knowing how the existing water level relates to the normal pool level enables the angler to determine the current feeding response of the bass.

King Of The Predators

The full-grown muskellunge may be "king" of the freshwater aquatic hill, but until it reaches about 15 inches it is still fair game for other predator fish, including bass.

Inch for inch, the largemouth bass is probably the most aggressive predator that swims, and muskies had better not get in the way! Actually, more muskies may end up in the stomachs

Live bait is vulnerable when hooked, and the bass realizes the bait's movements are constrained. Baitfish limitations caused by injury, fatigue or restricting cover create an opportunity for bass to strike.

of bass than vice versa. The West Virginia Department of Natural Resources reports that one collection of spotted bass for stomach analysis revealed several fat and happy muskie eaters. One spotted bass, less than a foot long, contained seven 6-inch muskies in its rather bloated stomach.

The sampling was taken the night after a stocking of fingerling muskies in the Bluestone Reservoir. Three other spotted bass taken for stomach analysis contained seven muskies, proving that this was no fluke.

Bass are aggressive predators. I, for one, am glad they are.

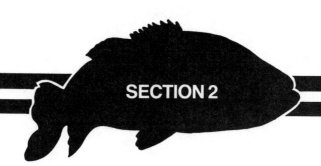

Where To Find Bass

5

Mapping Lore

Successful NAFC members can develop sound bass fishing strategies using topographical maps—if they know what to look for. The information you glean from a good topo map helps you catch more fish. Many successful professional bass tournament anglers firmly believe in topo maps and use them frequently to get a strategic reading on unfamiliar waters.

Many pro anglers travel extensively throughout the United States and fish several bass tournament circuits. While visiting each tournament site on their schedule, they will probably put thousands of miles on their vehicles and trailers. When they get to the lakes, they don't necessarily want to do the same to their boats.

Professionals like Larry Nixon, Harold Allen, Randy Fite and Ron Shearer minimize boat travel and develop productive bass-catching patterns quickly by utilizing topographical maps to locate bass-holding areas. Each of these anglers places a high value on good topo maps.

Larry Nixon feels it is most important to use a topo map at the time of year when the fish are on drops or breaks. The Hemphill, Texas, guide and tournament pro looks for contour lines that come extremely close together on a topographical map. Nixon has won several big-money tournaments on unfamiliar waters around the country thanks to his ability to interpret topo maps.

Tight Lines

"The closest contour lines on a map indicate sharp drop-offs and points—areas that attract fish," says Nixon. "When you have a good idea as to the depth and type of water the bass are holding in, you can develop a good pattern using a topo map.

"It doesn't have to be a great depth change," he continued, "just anywhere those contour lines come together and provide a change—at the back of a pocket or out on a point. Even the smallest change, from three to six feet, if it's a sharp drop, will hold concentrations of bass. On points, I look for a channel coming near the shallows.

"When lands are cleared prior to the filling of a reservoir, the cutting crews avoid the hard-to-get-to areas and saw off trees they can reach, leaving stumps," says Nixon. "Bass relate to these areas. Most can be located with a good map. You can also locate roadbeds, points, underwater bridges, fencelines or old tree rows. Bass relate to a change in water depth wherever the sharpest drop-off occurs.

"There might be a road ditch paralleling the tree line and an old creek crossing the ditch," adds Nixon. "Usually that type of area is the place you're looking for on topo maps."

A topo map shows you the coves and creeks that have definite channels. Nixon says these are very important in the springtime when you're looking for concentrations of fish. Such breaks may offer bass a migration route. A flat cove or pocket without a channel in it will normally have very few fish, according to Nixon.

"Flat areas can be good in the spring, though," he says. "Areas with greatly separated lines are often spawning flats. The best maps reveal little ditches or ridges in the flat areas and there might be more than 10 or 15 fish concentrated there. A large flat area that makes for good spawning ground might have a ditch or channel leading to outside drops or ridges where even more fish may be concentrated."

Pro Harold Allen of Batesville, Mississippi, agrees.

"The majority of bigger fish spawn in deeper water," he says. "After the spawn, they migrate to the outside of the flat and bunch up on points and knolls. When they're in the shallows they'll be scattered, but on a point they'll be schooled, and the odds of hitting the mother lode are better!

Bass professional Larry Nixon feels that the most important time of year to use a topo map is when the bass are on the drops or breaks in deep water.

Mapping Lore

"When bass move out to these points, they may not be hitting so you'll have to fish grubs or small lures," advises Allen. "When they get active, crankbaits get them and you can make a killing. The average fisherman, though, misses out on the action because he stays in shallow and keeps pounding the banks."

Seasonal Considerations

"The time of year is the main thing that tells us what to look for on a topo map," says Allen. "Knowing the time of year, we'll try to dissect the map. Deeper water just off a flat could be a good post-spawn or pre-spawn area.

"If a channel comes near a change in depth," he continues, "bass will use that for summertime activity. Bends in a deep channel are always good. The outside bends are slightly deeper than the inside bends and may have more brush—and fish!

"A depthfinder comes in handy to sort this out. Bass move up and down channels until they find the kind of water that's good for them. Water depth constantly changes along channels. A fish looks for something different along a break. The best areas combine good structure, deep water and flats.

"I look for little areas that are different and not so obvious," says Allen. "That's my edge and maps give that to me."

Maps reduce the amount of time needed to find fish, but they don't eliminate boat searches entirely.

"You can find many good-looking areas on a topo map, but you still need to take the time to check them out once you're on the water," he observes. "There could very well be some great spots that the map doesn't show, like a little ditch that cuts across a point or a brush-filled hole. The fish could be stacked in those locations.

"If you fish deep structure, you also have to run in and fish the obvious stuff that the bank chunkers are fishing," notes Allen. "In the limited time that most tournament fishermen have, we must also fish the obvious deep-water structure found on the topo maps."

Coloring The Lines

Randy Fite is well known for his bass locating abilities. The Montgomery, Texas, guide and professional fisherman is an

Harold Allen studies his topo maps for something that's not obvious to other anglers. Here he is working a breakline away from the more obvious timber.

Mapping Lore

expert at interpreting flashers, graphs and topo maps. He believes that choosing the right map is extremely important.

"Always get the best map available, one that has the detailed contour lines on it," he advises. "Sometimes I color those contour lines so that they are very easy to see at a glance.

"Once you get on a lake and develop a pattern (fish are at 25 feet and holding on sharp breaks, for example), pull out the map and follow the 25-foot contour line until it comes closest to a 40-foot contour line." He continues, "That indicates a sharp, vertical drop from the crest of 25-foot water and a good area! If you color code the lines, you speed up the process of finding similar locations.

"As far as looking for particular structures on topo maps, keep in mind your seasonal patterns," says Fite. "Summer structures appear relatively flat or gradually sloping. I look for lines that are far apart.

"In the winter time, I look for steep, vertical drops. The topo contour lines for these places will be very close together. You usually find structure around the major creek channels or out on the major river channels. These are usually the best areas to fish in cold-water situations."

Irregular Features

Professional bass angler and TV show host Ron Shearer firmly believes in the value of topo maps. He studies them to locate structure when fishing unfamiliar waters.

"I've yet to see a summer tournament that wasn't won by structure fishing," comments Shearer. "Structure is any irregular feature on the bottom or on the bank. You find the best summertime structure is usually out in the middle of the lake, and topo maps will help you locate it.

"In every hot-weather tournament, you can just lay a map down and pinpoint the spot where it was won," says Shearer. "That's always the case.

"Often, you won't catch a fish until you know what's there," says Shearer. "A map reveals detail about the area that would take hours to learn in a boat. First, I look for contour lines that are close together with fingers sticking out or indentions coming in. Then, I figure out how deep it is.

"I remember one time I marked all the fingers on a topo

Randy Fite color codes the contour lines on his topo maps to help speed up the process of finding identical structure.

map that didn't indicate the depths," Shearer laughs. "When I got to the lake, about half of them were out of the water, on ridge tops. You also have to know the depth so you don't mark creek channels that are 125 feet deep.

"Learning to use topographical maps is by far the easiest way to catch fish," he explains. "Catching bass is like putting together a puzzle. The map gives you an outline, but you have to put the rest of the pieces together."

====== 6 ======

Water Elimination

U nfamiliar waters challenge tournament professionals
and NAFC members alike. Huge impoundments
seemingly offer an endless variety of potential bass
haunts. Locating them is the problem.

Faced with overwhelming choices of habitat and prospective
patterns on unfamiliar water, successful touring anglers must
limit their fishing time to the most productive areas and
methods. There is little time to experiment with various lures or
to thoroughly check out a vast number of locations before a
tournament. Few professionals guess right about the best spot to
fish and the most productive technique to use. All agree that
you must first eliminate the majority of water available.

The angler who most effectively culls acres of water has a
good chance at winning the tournament. The ability to
eliminate the unproductive areas quickly separates successful
professionals from most other contenders in a tournament
situation. Knowing some of those ways should benefit NAFC
members or anyone who spends limited time on a large body of
water.

Tournament winners like Ken Cook, Ron Shearer, Tommy
Martin, Rick Clunn and Woo Daves all effectively eliminate
water. They make wise use of valuable time when they fish
waters relatively new to them. They've learned to concentrate
their practice time on potentially productive habitat. They
constantly learn, whether they catch fish or not. Winning

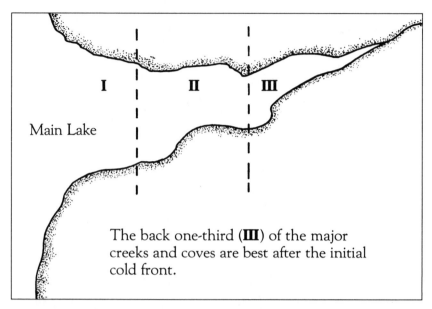

I | II | III

Main Lake

The back one-third (**III**) of the major creeks and coves are best after the initial cold front.

Rick Clunn's intimate knowledge of seasonal patterns helps him eliminate the front two-thirds of a major creek or cove during a fall cold front, for example.

tournament titles requires such abilities, and these guys have them.

Water Quality And Habitat

"I look for what seems the best bass-holding habitat in the lake," says Cook. "I often fall back to less quality habitat, though, if the best is too obvious and gets all the fishing pressure."

Cook considers type of cover, water color, chemistry (such as pH) and temperature in his elimination and selection process. His Multi-C-Lector, which identifies water pH, temperature and clarity values, plays a significant part in that process. He culls waters with visibility outside an optimal range of 15 to 24 inches.

Cook believes good habitat such as trees, bushes, rocks, grasses and drop-offs is necessary for good water quality. He says water that is not too clear and not too muddy is ideal.

Cook also eliminates water without a greenish tint. The greenish color guarantees a good base for the food chain, according to the former fisheries biologist. And, since bass are

Rick Clunn will sectionalize a map. Then, he'll concentrate on his seasonal patterns developed over years of experience.

Water Elimination

the top predators in this chain a good base is necessary to produce much at the top. He also eliminates waters with either consistently low or consistently high pH values.

"Once I eliminate most areas of the lake and settle on the one area that I believe to be best, I start fishing and evaluating the available cover types," says Cook. "I look for the type the bass prefer at the time, emphasizing the not-too-obvious cover. My basic goal is to quickly eliminate cover types that don't hold fish."

Cover Concentration

Ron Shearer also looks for places that are conducive to holding concentrations of largemouth. The pro doesn't like to spend a lot of time fishing a spot where he can't fish a school of bass. He's not fond of constantly moving about to pick up an isolated bass or two.

Shearer quickly eliminates places that would obviously hold only one or two fish, like logs scattered along a bank. Many people go in and catch a couple of bass, and no more, from that cover. Such anglers do not really establish a good pattern and probably hinder more than help their chances of catching numbers of fish.

"I try to eliminate as many places as I can that don't hold a school of bass," Shearer says. "Poor water color in a creek reveals that the pH is off, making bass inactive, so I'll move on. If you're on a gin-clear lake and it's time for the bass to be out on the ledges, you have to cull those creeks."

The bearded Kentuckian, however, keeps several back-up spots in mind, those holding only a bass or two, when tournament day rolls around. During practice rounds, he establishes the productive holes and also looks the lake over for other obvious fish-holding spots. He likes to know where they are so that he can utilize his tournament time efficiently if he finds unproductive practice holes.

Rick Clunn eliminates 75 percent of the lake before he even sees it. He sections off a lake and then relies on seasonal patterns to put him in its most productive area for that time of year.

"In the fall, my seasonal patterns tell me to concentrate on the backs of the creeks, preferably the major creeks," Clunn

Ron Shearer eliminates waters that don't hold a school of bass. He usually avoids small shoreline structure that holds only one or two fish.

says. "Now I only worry about these areas when I get to the lake. That gives me a much better chance of locating bass in a limited amount of time than if I went to the lake with the intention of fishing 20,000 acres."

Pattern Establishment

Tommy Martin feels that NAFC members have no shortcuts in eliminating water. First, they must develop a pattern quickly, he contends.

"Once you establish a pattern and determine the depth of water, type of cover and clarity of water in which you catch bass," he says, "you quickly eliminate areas of the lake that probably won't produce any bass, at least not with your established pattern.

"Keep in mind, though," Martin warns, "there can be a number of patterns or ways to catch bass within a given day. On most lakes during tournaments I try to establish at least two and sometimes three patterns using different lures. If one plays out, I have other options to try.

"The only way I feel really satisfied in eliminating water is

Tommy Martin relies on fast-moving lures like spinnerbaits to quickly eliminate a lot of water.

to fish that water with several different types of lures," says Martin. "To cover water faster, I use fast-moving lures, such as crankbaits and spinnerbaits. I fish until I'm satisfied there aren't enough bass in the area to catch."

The professional angler from Hemphill, Texas, however, stops and fishes key cover with a worm or a jig if he feels conditions warrant further exploration. He wants to see if there are bass in the area that wouldn't strike a fast-moving lure.

Blue Sky Analysis

Martin also says he quickly eliminates water by flying over a lake. He looks for water color differences and depth variations. He culls those areas that are either extremely shallow or muddy.

Woo Daves, a pro from Chester, Virginia, agrees with Martin.

"One of the most important and fastest means of water elimination is taking an airplane ride over the body of water you will be fishing," says Daves. "You see so much from the air that is very helpful, even on your home lake."

Daves looks first at the water conditions—clear, stained or muddy. Then he searches for the type of cover he's comfortable fishing. There is usually a lot of dead water (water with low oxygen content) in lakes and rivers that is easy to spot from the air, according to Daves. If a lake has clear, stained and muddy water, he fishes in the stained water or on the breakline where stained or muddy water meets clear.

"Next, I look for the right water temperature," he adds. "In the spring, the warmest water usually produces best. In summer it's the coolest. Many times in the spring just a couple of degrees makes all the difference between a big catch and nothing."

On unfamiliar lakes, Daves looks for the type of cover he's used to fishing. Usually he establishes a pattern.

"Find the cover you like to fish with the right water color and temperature and you are in business," he says.

In the spring, he concentrates on the larger feeder creeks, starting at the mouth and working back. In summer, Daves fishes main lake points and underwater structure. In the fall, he moves back to major feeder creeks, and then as the weather cools he fishes the smaller creeks.

Another key point when eliminating water is baitfish, according to Daves. Generally, if there are a lot of baitfish in an area bass are also there. He once fished Kerr Reservoir and found the water color, temperature and cover the same, but one particular area held a lot of baitfish.

"We fished one creek for 10 minutes and caught five or eight bass, left to fish identical cover (but without baitfish) for an hour or two and only caught one or two fish," says Daves. "This lasted for two days. We caught more than 50 bass in one creek while we caught only four bass outside of the creek, even though we fished the exact places in which we caught bass on past trips.

"Before going to a new lake, I try to get a good topo map and study it, call local fishermen to get their input and read any articles I can find on the lake," says Daves. "The more you know before you get there, the quicker you can pinpoint the fish."

According to Daves, it's just like taking a test in school. The more you study, the better you're going to do.

7

Natural Lakes

M ost of the natural lakes in North America are fairly shallow and usually somewhat round. That's not bad! The shallower a lake is, the easier it is for dissolved oxygen to penetrate the entire depth of the lake.

The roundness of a natural lake determines how the wind affects its stratification. On a round lake, wind from any direction creates wave turbulence and stirs up the lake into a more homogeneous body. You seldom find pockets of dead water in these shallow lakes.

No matter how much NAFC members prefer to fish on wind-protected waters, the fact is, a healthy, natural lake generally has very little wind protection. Fishing shallow, natural waters can sometimes be tough for that reason, but you can use the wind to your advantage while working good fish-holding structure.

Many anglers make a big mistake in assuming that shallow waters have only flat bottoms. Natural lake bottoms throughout the country abound with drop-offs, sunken islands, rock outcroppings, springs, fallen trees and creek beds. Since such structure provides food and cover for bass, understanding how to recognize good structure is important for consistent fishing success. The problem in fishing most natural waters is that there are just too many great-looking spots.

One of the most important things an NAFC member can do

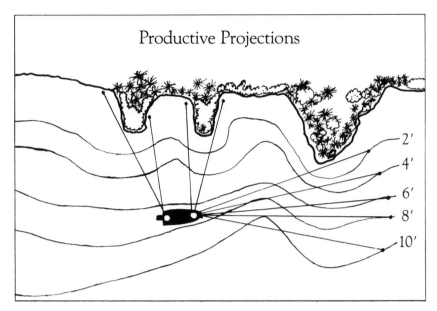

Productive Projections

2'
4'
6'
8'
10'

Natural lakes often have small protrusions. When working such points, cast as far back into them as you can and retrieve the lures parallel and as tight to the edges as possible. Work the longer points at various depths starting with casts to the shallower breakline.

when fishing a natural lake is learn to read the water and establish a pattern. The surface provides many keys to bottom structure. Shallow lakes are, by nature, weedy and generally have some sort of distinct weedline. Work the weedline points before any other portion of the weeds. Forget about working the entire weedline and start looking at the shore. Many times the shoreline definition provides a good indication of an area to search.

Thoroughly explore small pockets in heavy cover such as grass, bullrushes or lily pads, which can be excellent in natural lakes. Bass prefer the scattered light in these areas. Try to toss small lures into such places without creating a disturbance. Too much commotion in a small pocket of water frightens fish away.

In the spring, bass congregate back inside a shallow weedline. After spawning they generally move to the weedline nearest a drop-off and set up home for the summer.

Weed Ways

Bass frequent shallow weeds in the spring to spawn, but once they finish bedding, you can still find them in these waters

In relatively shallow natural lakes, bass can hold in thicker vegetation all day. The thick cover provides the bass with low light intensity, protection and cooler water temperatures.

for some time, depending on food availability and water clarity. Shallow, sparse weeds in deep, clean lakes may not hold many fish for long, while a tannic-acid-stained lake may have post-spawners in extremely shallow waters most of the year.

Both forage numbers and water clarity help you determine how long post-spawn bass in natural waters stay in the shallows. The weedier the water, the better its chance of holding a good population of bass. Also, the shallower the lake, the more apt bass will be to take up residence in the thickest bed of aquatic plants available.

Many weedy, natural lakes in the South have shallow-water inhabitants most of the year. Bass may move from shallow beds in two feet of water to heavy vegetation in about three feet of water and go on a post-spawn feeding binge for a couple of weeks. Then they move to the edges of heavy weedbeds (in four or five feet of water) and remain there for several weeks before moving to any deep-water structure that may be present.

You can find weed-infested natural waters in all areas, and most states have their share. The winter weather knocks the weeds down quickly, but they come back again in the spring or

Natural Lakes   79 early summer. An April day may be just too early to find lily pads at a location where a huge bed of bonnets existed the fall before. Consequently, some of the better weed fishing takes place in the late spring just after the spawn.

In some natural waters of southern states, weeds grow throughout the year. A mild winter increases the possibility of year-round weed fishing. In some states, the best time to fish natural lakes is in the spring and early summer. After that, the weed blanket may be just too heavy to penetrate with a lure.

Members of the NAFC should never overlook a natural lake full of moss or algae. Try fishing these waters in the springtime before the moss grows and clogs up access. Many natural waters get so overgrown with moss or weeds that there is only a small area in which to fish. A topwater plug or shallow-running lure that can be retrieved over the moss works best.

Poor water clarity shouldn't keep you from trying a lake. I do much of my fishing in waters with low visibility. Try these waters during droughts or after periods of several days with no rainfall. Most are clearer before spring rains and should produce best then.

Wade Back Alleys

Many natural waters have three distinct weedlines: one where the shoreline weeds end and two on either side of a bar that skirts the perimeter. Thus, a weedbed lies in front of the shore-based weeds, leaving a small channel between the two. This is usually a deeper trough bordered by sparse weeds.

Bass move along these alleys in search of forage. The edges are productive spots to cast, but wade fishing is most effective. Pockets of open water lie off to either side of the alley. The successful wader works these areas slowly and very thoroughly, hitting all irregular features.

As natural lake waters rise and cover the shoreline vegetation they produce similar areas, leaving those taller weed masses just offshore. These areas produce particularly well on windy days when waves pound the front face of the weedbeds. Largemouth often lie behind the windbreak in the shore weeds facing into the wind.

Successful waders look for stained water, hard bottoms and other structural changes that draw bass. They cast to the shallow side of any weed mass. They work the trough and pockets just off the mass by moving to the best casting spot. Lure presentation is a key to filling a stringer from the back alley.

Tough Stuff Strategy

Many NAFC members may pass up the tough stuff and miss out on some exciting bass fishing. Do you spend more time hung up than working the lure? Vegetation in natural lakes poses problems for many shallow-water anglers and sometimes means frustrating fishing. Those who learn to master the techniques for bass fishing natural waters, however, reap great rewards!

Snag-infested waters scare off many anglers who fear casting into the middle of the stuff. Many feel that it is too much work; others feel the chance of losing big fish in the slop is too great. Bass dwell in this heavy aquatic growth, though, and knowing how to successfully fish for them while preventing most hang-ups helps you catch more fish.

Spinnerbaits are very popular in the troughs and on the weedline. The bait should tip the weeds. This often triggers a strike from nearby bass. Floating, do-nothing and swimming worm rigs all produce. Small alleys and pockets in shallow cover are ideal for working these slower, more distinct lures. Their buoyancy keeps them out of tangles and in the strike zone longer.

Lightweight lures top the list for most natural lake anglers. These include floating minnow plugs, small crankbaits, small grubs, rubber lures (worms and grubs) and little spinners. Shallow-water bass spook easily, so a soft-landing, slow-moving morsel is an NAFC member's best bet for success.

If the water is exceptionally clear, long rods help the fisherman avoid spooking the fish. With unusually clear water, this equipment gives an angler distance. Light lures, web-thin lines and long casts on natural waters help fishermen put more bass in the livewell.

Many natural lakes have soft, muck bottoms. You can't wade them. For that reason you can't use heavy weights on Texas-rigged worms or deep-running crankbaits. Many anglers familiar with such waters prefer a topwater lure.

Bass Behavior

In spring, as plant growth flourishes in natural lakes, pH levels rise and fishing generally becomes easier because bass behavior stabilizes (as the pH levels near their preferred ranges). When there is an abundance of sunlight and sufficient aquatic vegetation, the pH level becomes more alkaline. Clear waters often have high pH levels. Light penetrates deeper into the water and allows more vegetation to grow.

Correspondingly, much higher pH levels exist around weedbeds than in barren areas. Under windy conditions with uniform mixing of pH, the weedbed itself should hold the highest levels of pH. Bass respond to these conditions by holding tighter to the weedbed.

You normally find natural lakes in areas with high levels of rainfall. Heavy showers in the summer or fall affect the fishing. Too much rain often increases the pH to a higher level than normal, causing bass to stop eating. The flushing of any shoreside bayous slows fishing on the lake's fringes.

Natural waters don't have all the large bass. Impoundments and reservoirs have their share, too. The two areas are alike in some ways and vastly different in others.

8

Shallow Impoundments

hallow reservoirs share some characteristics with deeper natural lakes. But you expend a lot of effort watching a depthfinder studying structure in waters less than 10 feet deep. If a contour plot or topographical map of the fishing area is not available, then make one. With a newly constructed contour map you gain an essential tool. You soon forget your tired eyeballs when a huge bass strains your tackle.

For NAFC members who don't have a depthfinder, wading is a particularly easy way to establish presence of structure and make your own topo maps of shallow waters. This is very refreshing in the summer months. Shallow-lake fishermen who don't have the patience to use a depthfinder can fish as they wade and cover a lot of ground.

I had some fabulous July fishing one year after wading a reservoir to define shallow bottom contours and establish a pattern. In fact, my brother, two friends and I caught several bass between 5 and 6 pounds that week.

Hot and muggy were two words to describe that week's weather. The daytime temperature highs ranged from 99 to 103 degrees. The heat and work commitments of the others allowed only for 8 a.m. to noon fishing hours.

We concentrated our efforts on the western half of a state-owned impoundment. This portion of the shallow reservoir had an underwater ridge running out into the lake and the acreage was half covered with stickups. Small dead and rotting trees inundated much of the area we were fishing.

We trailered a boat to the lake the first morning but soon decided to wade as that was an easier way to cover the area more thoroughly while obtaining facts for our contour maps. By necessity, we spent a lot of time that morning without catching bass. We were after topo readings first and bass second.

The lake bottom was mud, and with each step we sank into a few inches of silt. The lake had a maximum depth (in the western 70 acres) of about six feet. We found wading easy and the water helped cool us off. We all spread out and covered as much water as possible, taking notes and making observations on each weedbed, point or log where we found bass.

The muddy water had about one foot of visibility. We could see our lures descend about six inches into the murk before they disappeared. The naturally poor clarity allowed the bass to inhabit such a shallow lake and thus made a one-foot drop a great breakline.

Action Time

The four of us caught 53 bass that day. A pea-green Cordell "Big O" plug and a chartreuse spinnerbait worked the best that day and the next. We chose crank-type, vibrating baits due to the poor water clarity and a substantial wind.

The following day the four of us waded chest-deep in the murk searching for further facts. Inch-long shad cruised about the lake's surface. Periodically, a small bass would bust them on the surface. We caught several feeding bass by casting to the action. The shad soon disappeared and we continued our exploration and probing. We caught and released a total of 67 bass by noon.

As we drove home that afternoon, we tried to put it all together. We assembled a map that included all surface structure features such as stickups, posts, weeds and pads. From looking at that sketch we determined other potentially good areas. Without the contour plot, much of our time would have been wasted.

We added all depth data to the sketch in the form of contour lines. We noted three-, four- and five-foot depths. On the third morning, with our maps fairly complete, we concentrated on the lunker haunts. We totaled only 22 bass

Wade fishermen often find bass in the backs of shallow coves. They can thoroughly work the habitat from optimal positions.

that day, including four between 5 and 6 pounds. The next morning I took the largest, a 5½-pounder, and Ron landed a 4¾-pound largemouth. That day's total was 33 bass.

Final Analysis

The four of us landed 175 bass in four mornings. A dozen of them ranged from 4½ pounds to 6 pounds, and most of the others were 1 to 2 pounds. This is not spectacular by any means, but if we hadn't fished that shallow structure, our totals would have been minimal. Several other fishermen on the impoundment who probed deep-water areas caught few, if any, bass. That, along with the blistering heat, evidently established the "very poor" fishing report for this particular lake that week!

All but two of our lunkers came from a shallow point and along a trough. That's a pretty good breakline! Wading to establish the contours resulted in this find.

Shallow reservoirs similar to this one exist all over the United States. Good topo maps are available for only a few, so you must wade them or study a sensitive depthfinder to cover them. In either case, you often have to make your own map.

Take paper and pencil with you and rough out all surface structure such as pads, grass, trees, piers, stumps and rocks. Learn to read the water. Then make contour plots of all depths and get as much detail as you can. It'll mean a hefty reward in bass if you do your research.

Start Your Search

NAFC members who fish shallow reservoirs for the first time should take a systematic approach. Since most of us don't have all the time in the world, we should use it to our best advantage. Let's assume we will wade to establish our contours. Look over the shallow water for distinct points first. Many times, since the lake is shallow, the land surrounding it is fairly flat and the points are not as noticeable as on a deeper lake. There is almost always a point where a tributary enters the lake.

Enter the water here and slowly work your way into deeper water. Fan cast in all directions while moving slowly along the ridge of the sloping underwater point. Work all points starting at the upper end of the reservoir where the water is generally not as clear. As an alternative, you could fish the points on the windward side nearest the dam.

Shallow reservoirs can be weedy and may have some sort of a weedline. Hit the weedline points before looking at any other portion of the weeds. After that, forget working the entire weedline and just look at the shore. Many times the shoreline gives you a good indication of a prime area to search for structure, while the weeds in the lake may all look alike.

Submerged Structure

Scan the lake for submerged ridges or islands. Many times a weed growth, tree line or row of fence posts gives away the presence of an island or ridge. Wade both sides and establish contours along the entire ridge. Find the best breakline along this ridge and mark it on your map. The edges of the drop-off closest to deep water should be the most productive.

Explore these areas thoroughly. They can be utopias in a shallow reservoir. Bass move along them as they search for forage. All fish prefer the scattered light in these areas.

Points are the most productive areas in shallow reservoirs for largemouth bass hiding in submerged brush and trees. Map the

outside edge contour of such points first. If you wade and fish, take care not to step on the brush or trees. Snapping off limbs while you stomp through the area scatters the bass.

Many times, NAFC members literally stumble onto super structure while wading standing timber. Submerged stumps often hold bass. The outer edge of the shallow-water timber should be productive, especially if it butts deeper water. For future trips, note depths where you encounter action.

Continue Your Search

Once you read the lake, cover all likely looking areas and plot their contours on your structure map, you are ready to cover open water. This can be tiring but is often well worth the effort.

Several holes that contain many bass may exist in the open areas on shallow impoundments. When you find a hole, check out the depth thoroughly after fishing it and try to locate a drop-off containing underwater structure. All holes are potentially productive in shallow reservoirs since dissolved oxygen penetrates most depths.

Shallow structure can hold as many fish as structure in deeper water, so work it thoroughly.

Shallow Impoundments

When it's cold and the sky is clear, start on the windward side of a reservoir where the dissolved oxygen is highest. Most heavy vegetation holds heat and this makes such areas very productive.

I've caught bass in two to two and a half feet of water on the windward side of a lake. Fish won't feed much in cold water because their metabolism slows. Head to the warmest waters you can find. The temperatures in many reservoirs vary from one side to the other by as much as 10 to 15 degrees.

Once you plot all the contour lines in the shallow water you fish, you'll have a valuable tool for all seasons. Shallow waters are less predictable than the deeper lakes when the weather changes, but they are not impossible. With your new contour map, you'll eliminate several fishless areas.

A contour map is just as important when fishing a shallow reservoir as when fishing a deeper one. Shallow-water structure can hold as many fish as structure in deeper water. With your homemade map in hand, you'll have a head start on locating the lunkers.

=====9=====

Ponds And Potholes

S mall ponds are everywhere, and many of them offer excellent bass fishing. The key is finding the best ponds, which is difficult to do with a countryside full of good-looking waters. Knowing where to look and what to look for will help you with your search.

Most NAFC members probably see a number of small ponds or potholes from highways and backroads during their travels. There are many more hidden from the casual observer. Just how a pond is used has a direct bearing on how good the fishing might be. How it was intended to be used is also important. Ponds used primarily as water supply for livestock can vary greatly in fish productivity. Generally, the more livestock permitted access to a particular pond, the poorer its fishery will be.

Ponds used as a source of water for fire control or limited irrigation should be less disturbed and offer better fishing. Wide fluctuation brought on by heavy irrigation, however, harms the fishery. If the pond's sole purpose is to supply water for farm homes or create habitat for waterfowl and other game, it should provide some excellent fishing. Most ponds and their margins are natural with weeds and other wild growth aiding the filtering of their waters.

You can usually find the best fishing in a pond designed specifically for recreation. You should search these waters out. But you can often determine if the water is worth fishing before

Pond characteristics vary substantially, and it may be difficult to find all of the ideal conditions. Certain waters, however, will have enough of the right characteristics to provide plenty of bass action.

you charge up to a farmhouse and ask permission to fish a pond. You must learn to analyze pond characteristics such as drainage, physical dimensions, clarity, vegetation and construction.

Drainage Character

A pond or natural pothole is no better than its drainage area. This is the most important characteristic to analyze in the waters you wish to fish. Investigate the runoff areas above the lake and try to get some idea of the entire pond site.

If the drainage area consists of too much cultivated land, erosion results in partial silting. You must determine the size of the drainage area from the lay of the land. The actual water level gives you a good indication. If it appears shallow, the drainage area is too small. Such a pond could certainly dry up in the middle of the summer or in drought conditions.

The drainage area is too large if the pond usually fills to the brim and appears to be at flood stage much of the year. With such a large watershed area, excess water probably brings in too much silt, which disturbs the food chain. A surprisingly large amount of silt is deposited in farm ponds, even if they are surrounded by grassland pastures.

Better ponds have watersheds with grass or other types of permanent vegetation around them. This usually assures the water is clear enough to sustain a good fishery. If the drainage area is heavily crop-oriented, the pond could be full of silt. A loss of only 25 percent of water storage capacity can make a pond useless for fishing.

Physical Dimensions

Ponds of less than a half acre are usually too small to contain many sizable fish. Look for ponds with surface areas of three-quarters of an acre up to two or three acres. Larger waters are great for fish production, but they are not necessarily better than smaller ponds.

Pond sizes often depend largely on the amount of rainfall in the area. Other factors also interact to determine the size of the pond. Composition, type of soil and subsoil, the slope and the type of vegetation determine the available runoff.

When you find heavy fishing pressure on the ponds you are analyzing, try the largest pond. It is the best equipped to handle the pressure. According to fishery biologists, a pond can withstand a harvest of 50 pounds of fish per acre each year without hurting its ecosystem.

Analyze the depth of the pond by scanning the shore terrain. In general, water depths should be five feet or more for good bass production, especially in the North where ponds may freeze solid during the winter. If you find a rugged shoreline with steep banks and sharp points jutting out, it should have the depth needed to sustain a healthy bass population. If you find a mainly round pothole with no points or coves, check it out for adequate depth.

Many times you can tell the kind of fishery a man-made pond has by noting the construction of the dam or spillway. The ideal pond has a dam that is neither too narrow nor too steep. Observe how much erosion has occurred on the face of the dam. Erosion is a sure sign of a dam in trouble.

A good spillway is well-sodded and lies perhaps two feet below the top of the dam. If well-designed, the spillway will be located away from the dam (earth fill), not at one end of it. It should be designed to take water out in a wide sheet.

Pond Weeds

Some vegetation is needed, but too much in a shallow body of water may be undesirable. Weed growth often becomes so dense in clear, tiny waters that it offers too much protection for small fish. Too many cattails, water lilies and other plants can be as undesirable as a floating mat of scum or moss. Most NAFC members know ponds or potholes that are completely choked with aquatic plant life. The fishing is usually poor in such ponds.

Adequate vegetation actually reveals fertile waters. The growth of microscopic plant life and algae stimulates the growth of small animal forms, such as crustaceans and insect larvae, which feed on plant life. In the presence of an abundant food supply these tiny animal forms grow rapidly and provide food for small fish. The small fish, in turn, serve as forage for the larger predator fish we pursue.

In shallow waters with too much vegetation, there are other problems. In the late, hot summer, there is often a loss of fish. When the vegetation becomes mature and dies, the decomposition requires much oxygen, leaving the fish with less than they require.

An important characteristic of better ponds is relatively clear water. That water is cooler because it absorbs less sunlight, contains more oxygen and provides a more suitable habitat for most small organisms.

Extremely muddy water interferes with successful bass spawning. If the pond you have your eye on is muddy after rains and the condition continues for more than a week, cross it off your list. The soil in the runoff area could be heavily clay-based and minute particles carried into the pond during rain could remain in suspension, causing an almost permanent turbid condition.

Analysis And Aesthetics

NAFC members should analyze all characteristics of the pond to arrive at a valid conclusion. Certain waters are strong in some areas and weak in others. The perfect pond may not exist but you can find many close enough.

It's not always easy to launch your bass boat on small ponds, but some have improved boat ramps. Nice fish!

Ponds And Potholes   93

Ideal ponds show little water level fluctuation. The pond that I look for has: an adequate drainage area with permanent vegetation, a depth of at least eight feet, a sodded spillway and dam, a fence around the entire area, relatively clear water with visibility of two feet or more, adequate cover such as lily pads, stumps and rocks, and a water surface of 4 or 5 acres. Oh, and it should be stocked with Florida bass!

If aesthetics do anything for you, you'll find that the smaller ponds and potholes are generally prettier. Small natural ponds are frequently surrounded by trees, while others are located in the middle of farmland.

Some of these small ponds have boat ramps, but generally there are no fish camps or marinas here. You must often wade or else bring a small boat or float tube. I usually take my 8-foot Water Spider to these ponds. I sneak up on plenty of bass in most of these little-fished waters.

Similar Structure

Structure in shallow water affects bass the same way as structure in a deep lake. It's all relative.

I did most of my beginning bass fishing (in the late 1950s) in a shallow farm pond with barely six feet of water. This pond had what we now call structure. Several dead trees protruded from the muddy water, defining the old creek bed running through the pond.

In this five-foot creek bed I caught my first 7-pound bass. It was late spring and I was working a balsa plug along the brushiest tree at the creek bed's edge when the bass grabbed the lure. Partially submerged brush along the old creek channel formed the super structure for the acre pond's bass. All our good fish came from this area.

Prairie potholes are often isolated in a sea of submerged grass, but they can be bass fishing hotspots. A narrow, pointed craft, such as a square-stern canoe, is ideal for reaching such places. Cast into the nearest weed edges, but don't neglect the center of a small pothole. Worms (especially when rigged Texas-style) or spinnerbaits are fairly weedless for this type of angling and very productive. Quietly casting with a twitching injured-minnow plug often provides a chance at the biggest fish in the whole pond or pothole.

Remote waters often contain numerous small, keeper-size largemouth, and occasionally a trophy can be pulled from the lightly fished areas. A soft plastic worm rigged Texas-style is extremely productive in highly vegetated ponds.

Lure Selection

Ponds and potholes normally possess a smaller-sized forage base. Take this into account when selecting a lure. You may need to use shorter, thinner plugs in these waters to reap the best results. Prior to lure selection, you should consider the fishery composition and size of predominant forage. That's the advice from this believer of "big baits for big bass."

Accurate and careful casters can fish a pond with sparse cover with almost any weedless lure. In this category you just can't beat a soft plastic worm rigged slip-sinker style.

One of the best lures for fishing small ponds and potholes is the light, balsa wood minnow imitation. Since bass may be unaccustomed to seeing artificial lures in some potholes, they often strike at most types. The floating minnow-type plug has great action and is a strong producer. Fish this on top, just under the surface or with a combination of the two.

Many scoff at ponds and potholes due to their size. Yet they sometimes produce bigger bass than the much larger lakes nearby. Look at the state records and you generally find "private

Ponds And Potholes

pond" listed more than any other body of water. What more incentive do you need to try these little jewels?

Like ponds and potholes, marshes and swamps provide NAFC members with productive and often underfished sources of great bass fishing.

=10=

Marshes And Swamps

L ike ponds, the often hidden waters of marsh areas and small sloughs offer excellent fishing. Most seem to have no visible approach by deep water. One must often blaze a trail to these areas through underbrush and thick vegetation that may stand head-tall.

Members of the NAFC won't find a lot of people back in the shallow marshes because it often takes hard work to reach the right areas. There usually aren't many big bass in these clear waters either, but don't be surprised if you catch an occasional lunker. The majority of marsh bass weigh up to 2½ pounds.

Wildlife of all kinds thrive in the shallow marsh plain. In some areas you'll find alligators, raccoons, waterfowl, armadillos, bobcats, wild hogs, deer—and snakes. This is particularly important information for those of us who wade such areas or use very small boats. Fortunately my eight-foot Water Spider has an ample freeboard.

Marshlands exist all along the Gulf Coast and lower Atlantic. Marshes are usually present in the flood plain of most major river systems that empty into saltwater. Marsh, swamp and prairie potholes are typical of many natural lowland waters with difficult access.

Shallow, thin-draft, flatbottom boats are probably the best means of marsh transportation. Push, pole or pull them through the extremely shallow wet spots to reach slightly deeper, more productive waters.

Many wildlife refuges are marsh-like and require airboats or other special transportation to get to productive fishing areas. Good bass fishing exists in marshlands all along the coastal plains and in some major river systems that empty into saltwater.

Prairie Holes

West prairie marsh surrounds many pothole lakes. During normal water conditions the shallow prairie may be almost completely submerged. Some holes, with depths of six to eight feet, may be present for the adventurous explorer with a lightweight boat.

Grass in a prairie area is often, for the most part, impenetrable. Boat trails may exist in some areas, but they are useless in years of drought. During dry periods marsh holes are inaccessible to anglers, except perhaps those with four-wheel-drive swamp buggies. Many of these prairie holes haven't been fished for years and have huge bass waiting for the NAFC member who probes their depths.

Southern guides catch big fish from many open-water holes created by alligators. Since the early days, huge gators have burrowed their way through the shallow grass patches to their lakeside residences. This constant traffic keeps growth of aquatic vegetation down in some areas, forming small coves with water deep enough to support bass.

A marsh's irregular shoreline is often the result of alligator movement and bass love this "custom-built" terrain. The alligators themselves seldom cause anglers problems. Good numbers of the reptiles inhabit the swampy prairies of the Deep South, and I'm glad. They create numerous bass fishing opportunities.

Marsh Compartments

Freshwater marshes are often compartmentalized. Bass fishing within these compartments can be excellent during high-water periods. The water level can be manipulated by control structures in some levees. A periodic drawdown is often used to control aquatic weed growth. When the gates open, the shallow portions of the marsh dry out and so does the bass fishing.

A refuge normally consists of impounded marshes and lagoons. The water may be brackish and is generally shallow. Waters in the interior of most refuges contain a good population of bass. Knowledgeable fishermen haul occasional lunkers up to 9 or 10 pounds from the swamps. Dikes with narrow car trails or paths winding over the refuge sometimes serve as points of access to marsh hotspots. These trails, usually built to aid duck hunters in reaching blinds, provide convenient bank spots for land-bound anglers.

Black-Water Swamps

Swampland waters can be very dark from the tannic acid emitted by cypress trees and other flora. In dark waters NAFC members can generally catch more fish. The poor water clarity covers up angler mistakes, and we all make them. Fish are usually closer to the surface, which allows fishermen a better chance at fooling some of them. Since most fishermen are better "catchers" in shallow water, this is their opportunity to battle some fish in the low-visibility waters.

Reeds, along with fallen timber or brush in three to four feet of water, are other prime spots. Dark waters produce particularly well in spring and fall. The edges of lily pads and water hyacinths are springtime haunts of largemouth bass.

During winter, colder surface water temperatures drive bass deeper. The low-visibility water provides an insulation to the weather. Largemouth bass remain shallower in darker waters. Don't overlook dark water when the weather cools. Put your lure in but be careful. Something may just take it away from you.

Finding Remote Waters

While fishing any area that has numerous connecting bodies of shallow water, certain things help me find the better spots. An important starting point is remote and out-of-the-way waters.

It may not be pleasant to trudge through several hundred yards of brush, trees or marsh grass to fish when there's a nice body of water right next to the parking lot. But believe me, it's worth it. The more remote and inaccessible the body of water, the less fishing pressure it gets. This holds true for all types of water.

To locate remote spots, I start by talking to other fishermen or people who live in the area. Sometimes a brief conversation can do more good than a day or two of running around and looking.

Another tip for NAFC members is to get up on a high spot of some type and survey the area looking for water off the beaten path. A friend once climbed a water tower to view a marsh area for new hotspots. From his observation point he noted several nice swamps that appeared slightly deeper than the other ponds in the area. A few had no noticeable approach even by water. He had to blaze a trail through underbrush and seven-foot-tall rushes. An even tougher part of his trek later that day was carrying out several bass from the hidden marsh.

Marsh Methods

To catch a nice string of bass from a remote swamp or marsh, keep several things in mind. If the water is very cold, as it usually is in the spring, and warm southerly breezes have been blowing all week, you may find an area of warm water on one side of the lake. This is the place to fish.

If a stiff wind has been blowing across a shallow marsh, baitfish will probably be on the side where the waves have been hitting. Strong winds slowly push the surface water across the marsh and warm it in the cooler months. The whitecaps

Shallow swamps are often crammed with lily pads, which provide the necessary ingredients for some exciting bass fishing. Lily pads may be the only cover in these neglected waters. Successful anglers can avoid the crowds and catch plenty of bass by learning how to fish marsh waters.

oxygenate the water and carry baitfish to keep the gamefish from starving.

Generally, the shallower marsh banks warm up most quickly because they are easily penetrated by the sun.

A Cut Above

A dike bordering a marsh or swamp often defines a canal system on that side. If run-outs from the marsh can be found every 100 yards or so, that's an ideal situation.

These cuts are especially good when the water is moving. This happens after a rain overflows the marsh into the bayous and canals or when the swamplands are extremely low and water is sucked into the canals. The latter occurs when tide or floodwaters run full-bore and the canal system's level decreases to a point well below that of the marsh.

Any source of freshwater is a prime marsh spot and usually a great place to find feeding gamefish. Food, oxygen, cooler water and bass are all present in most runoff situations and remote swampwaters usually have plenty of each.

Marshes And Swamps

Currents are influenced by freshwater influx and by the marsh's outflow. If there is a heavy influx and good outflow the current should also be healthy. As the current moves it pushes and pulls at the water sitting in the marsh, causing some turbulence. Weaker forage specimens get swept out of the extremely shallow areas.

Rainfall, irrigation pumps, locks or other causes of intermittent flow have a great effect on the feeding of lowland bass. The angler who takes advantage of a drain situation, whether it's a runoff or a pull (suction of water), often finds exceptional largemouth angling. I have fished these areas at the right stage and have quickly taken limits of schooling bass.

NAFC members will find successful marsh bass fishing at night. If snakes, gators and other "scrams in the dark" bother you while you're in a boat or wading, night fishing may not be for you. Make sure your equipment is in good working order before you venture into such areas after dark.

When you're fishing dark swampwater, remember that feeding fish do not rely on sight as much as they do in clear water. You must cast near them to entice a strike. A toss landing two feet away from a swirl (denoting the presence of a bass) may not attract it. Casting the lure right on top of the spot may.

Topwater lures fished slowly in waters of limited visibility are productive. In moving water the lures can be worked faster against the current. An erratic retrieve is best then.

Fishing in the remote marsh waters can be better than in other, more accessible spots. The natural beauty is usually unspoiled. All anglers should try to keep it that way while enjoying some fantastic bass fishing.

=11=

Probing Pit Diggings

Thousands of watercraft are car-topped and trailered to man-made bass waters such as mine and borrow pits each year. Lightweight rigs are particularly suited to the pits, which seldom have a launch ramp. A trolling motor is generally sufficient to maneuver.

Man-made waters are abundant in many areas, yet they receive little attention. Irrigation canals, borrow pits dug for highway fill, and small reservoirs may provide great shallow-water bass fishing. An angler can often double his catch rate in such waters. Bass there seem to grow faster and chunkier.

These often-overlooked waters aren't pretty, but they may be stocked naturally and filled with largemouth. I like to fish places like this due to the lack of angling pressure. I've often found hungry fish and quick limits.

Most pits have an irregular shoreline. Waters are of medium clarity, but occasionally you find a pit with fairly clear water. Many have rocks, sand and gravel outcroppings.

Bass quickly adapt to unique pit structures. Brush structure is usually abundant along the lake bottom. Vegetation may grow profusely before a pit is flooded. Once inundated, the vegetation provides excellent cover for the entire food chain, from phytoplankton right on up to largemouth bass.

Lunker hunters concentrate on this terrain to harvest big bass. Many pits in the South have produced bass more than 14 pounds, but seldom does the word get out as to which pit

Crankbaiting shallow pit structures is a highly effective method for catching big bass during cool periods, as the author's parents found out. The two fish pushing 14 pounds in total were "cranked" out of hydrilla cover on two quick passes.

produced the lunker. The lucky anglers are usually pretty tight-lipped.

Mining Treasures

Most pits result from mining operations. Thousands of miniature bass factories have been created around the country after rock deposits are unearthed to provide raw material for various end products. In Florida, for example, a number of fabulous phosphate pits exist in Polk County, which is between Tampa and Orlando. Many pits also exist in other states.

The phosphate industry was once openly criticized for "scarring" the landscape. It now enjoys a different reputation. Large mining and processing firms lead the way in creating new bass waters and restoring those pits that have been dug.

Mining companies follow stringent government regulations as they reclaim the land. Nature does its share of the work to vegetate shorelines and existing islands, creating excellent habitat for the food chain that normally blossoms in the highly enriched waters. Many of the pits are stocked, while others prosper thanks to wading birds that pick up eggs on their feet in one pond and transfer them to a second.

Structure Galore

When huge dragline buckets dig through soil to get to the rock beneath, they often create dead-end channels, islands and a multitude of structure and depth changes. A single scoop of a massive bucket leaves a hole large enough for a three-bedroom house. The depth of these waters varies from site to site, but NAFC members should focus on the shallows.

When the mining operations cease, the holes are filled with water. The lakes that result contain underwater humps and other projections above the water surface. Water clarity varies depending on shoreline characteristics, the drainage land and the degree of water manipulation through the pits.

Bass pits in most states vary from a couple of acres up to 500 or so. All of the pits have different structure. Some have vast pad beds, others have cattails and bullrushes and still others are nearly devoid of emergent vegetation. Some of the better pits even have a profuse growth of hydrilla. Many have sharp drop-offs near their banks while other pits have small hills on their perimeters.

There may be a thousand different types of shoreline on little man-made waters. The better ones have deep water nearby and some structural characteristics for the bass to migrate along to the shallow bank. The vegetation just off deep water is a good place to begin searching for bass.

Forage is often shallow in pits and predators move to it. Big bass bury themselves in the heavy cover and await their prey. Bluegill, golden shiners, shad and other baitfish species are present in most pits throughout the South. Pit bass generally prefer the thin-shaped shad or shiner forage. Other popular treats for hungry largemouth are the crayfish that frequent the numerous rocks found in most pits.

Water levels vary in pits connected to a chain of lakes. Control structures often regulate these levels. Spillways and culverts with flowage are hotspots for feeding bass. The bottom is generally carved out beneath such discharges, and hungry largemouth may lie off to the side of the fast water in four- to six-foot depths facing the current.

Submerged islands are excellent places for bass to corner hapless prey. Cuts in the islands are excellent spots to fish because the largemouth generally lie off such areas awaiting a school of baitfish.

Wintertime lure presentations should be slow as bass are somewhat sluggish. The real heavyweights come from thick cover or off submerged structure on such retrieves. They are often in stuff so thick that they have a limited view. Submerged brush and rock provide a sanctuary to many lunker pit bass.

I usually fish any pit shoreline habitat or offshore shallow cover with crankbaits or plastic worms. Then I look at depth changes, which often requires some investigation. If I'm without a depthfinder, I use a tailspinner lure or ⅜-ounce slip sinker in front of a worm to figure out depths. Crankbaits that run to seven or eight feet are adequate for similar evaluation of the bottom terrain.

My normal six-hour fishing day on a pit usually results in 10 to 15 bass, which is well above my average production on most other types of water. The Florida Game and Fresh Water Fish Commission verified through creel samplings that pit fishing produces more than fishing natural lakes on a fish-per-hour basis.

Pit pH Factors

When the first pH meter came out several years ago I quickly learned its value on phosphate pits. My pH meter read 6.5 at the upper end of the pit near a crude dirt launch ramp. The water was only 20 inches or so deep for more than a quarter of a mile until I moved through a bend where several islands stood guard on a major portion of the machine-dug bass water.

The bottom dropped to six feet before I felt a need to toss a lure to the heavy cover growing at the pit's edge or around the attractive mid-lake lands. The pH reading was at 6.7 when I hooked my first bass. The following hours were slow with only two bass jumping at my crankbaits retrieved through a small stretch of muddy water. In that area the pH meter indicated a value of 6.8, the closest yet to the 7.5-to-7.9 reading considered optimal for feeding largemouth.

Finally, I had another strike and put the 3-pounder in the boat's aerated well. The pH meter read 7.0. That's a long way

Pit fishing is more productive in general than angling in many other types of water. If the pH is right, bank-bound anglers can get in on the action.

from 7.5 but on that pit it was the closest I had seen. And I had covered most of it. Could such a small difference in pH values make a difference in catch rate? It didn't take long to find out. Four casts later I had two chunky bass in the boat. Each catch was from the island and the 7.0 pH water.

High pH Levels

The experiment continued in another phosphate pit some four miles down the road. The 40-acre lake was open with no islands or heavy cover along its shore to slow down an increasing wind.

I began casting in the shallow water as I let the wind push the boat. After 20 minutes of fruitless casting the depth dropped to five feet. The pH level was 8.0 when the first largemouth from this pit hit a 7-inch blue worm. For the next 200 yards the action was nonstop until the windward shore became shallow and the action dwindled back to nothing. The pH climbed to a high mark of 8.4 in the final 100 yards of the float.

I slowly motored back to the beginning of the deep water where the meter read 8.0 and began another pass. Several chunky bass again strained my rod. After two more passes and 16 bass caught and released, I had time to check the other shoreline. I had drifted from the lee to the windward banks along only one shoreline.

I made two passes over the deep water on the other side, working shoreline identical to that across the lake. I was without a single strike but had learned something. The pH reading shot up to 8.9 in the apparently barren water. I returned to the opposite bank for a final drift and caught four more keeper-size bass.

Whereas the pH level in the first pit that I fished was uniformly below the 7.5-to-7.9 figure, the waters in the second pit had a range of 8.0 to 8.9. I found that the closer the pH to the preferred range, the better the bass angling.

The pH factor in shallow water is likely to change drastically during the course of a day. Photosynthesis increases the pH of water. Other factors alter it on cloudy days and after the sun goes down. For bass, look for water with good habitat that is closest to pH 7.5 to 7.9, whether it is above or below this range.

Pit bass are active year-round. Water temperatures are usually conducive to feeding fish, which makes the angling easier. Man-dug waters provide a variety of cover, and you can generally find the hot action by angling from a small boat or by casting from the banks.

=12=

Rivers, Creeks And Run-Ins

S hallow rivers and creeks throughout the country have received an unfair reputation as being sparsely populated, small bass waters. But heavyweight bass can be found in tributaries of all sizes, and productive methods unique to these waterways aid both the quality and quantity of an angler's catch.

Successful angling techniques used on natural lakes and reservoirs won't always work in a river environment, which is constantly in motion. Current dictates a slightly different approach to finding and catching the largemouth bass. Habitat orientation and bait or lure presentation take on significant meaning in moving waters. Consideration of each is vital to the successful river angler.

River systems throughout the country are finally generating some interest among the bass fishing fraternity. The St. Lawrence River in New York, the Arkansas River in Arkansas, the Alabama River in Alabama and the Kissimmee River in Florida have all achieved a modicum of publicity among bass anglers for significant bass catches.

In Florida alone there are approximately 1,700 streams. They range in size from small spring creeks to large rivers. Undoubtedly, more big largemouth bass are in the 318-mile-long St. Johns River than in any other. But thousands of lesser-known rivers and creeks throughout the country also produce big bass.

While some tributaries harbor bass that seldom see a lure, others receive heavy fishing pressure.

Specific techniques that produce in current conditions on one river often work well on others. Successful NAFC members learn to read the water and adapt their angling to a particular waterway.

Some rivers are comprised of demineralized, nutrient-poor waters. While these waters are not great producers of fish and plants, they may be chemically well-suited for a great bass fishery. These rivers often support very active populations of shallow largemouth that are relatively undisturbed by anglers.

Food Chain

One key to putting river bass in the boat lies in knowing the predominant forage available to them. The forage variety differs from that found in a natural lake or reservoir. Concentrations of favorite impoundment forage such as threadfin shad are seldom found in the smaller tributaries of the South, nor will you find them in northern rivers.

Rivers and creeks generally have a smaller food chain than lakes. You find fewer crappies, for example, but there are generally good numbers of sunfish. Shiners and other small minnow species often abound in moving waters. Crayfish are also more numerous in the rocky, sandy reaches of smaller tributaries than in mud-bottom lake waters.

Moving waters dictate lure selections that closely resemble the particular forage found in rivers and creeks. First, try to determine the forage most available in the particular river you are fishing; then match it as closely as possible to the lures you are using.

Jigs, spinners, small crankbaits, short plastic worms and rubber crayfish imitations generally produce. Weedless baits that are less likely to snag in a rocky crevice are also practical choices.

Lures that are easy to control in current are usually more productive. In some river situations, current pushes an unanchored craft at a fairly rapid rate, which restricts anglers to making only one or two casts per fish-holding structure. The successful angler must consider the water current, available forage and more when selecting a lure.

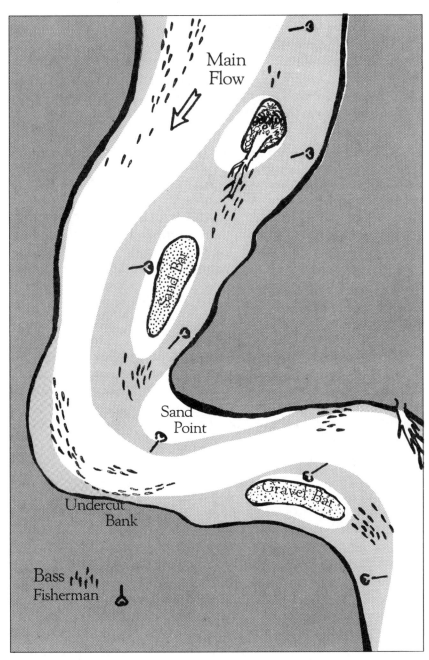

Rivers can offer a great bass fishery. Shallow streams even have ample depth for certain species of bass, and many are very wadeable. Try to pick out the prime river bass areas.

Current Considerations

While streams offer NAFC members a smaller area with better defined casting targets, they also force them to cope with moving water. Fish in shallow rivers are often concentrated. Only lures presented in close proximity to them will work. Casts must account for current movement in addition to that imparted by the angler.

Look for bass near trees or roads, or along riverbanks. Place your lure in the shallow rapids, riffles or other areas of rapid current, and you may catch a spotted, Guadalupe, redeye, shoal, Suwannee or smallmouth bass, depending on which state and waters you're fishing. For the ever-popular largemouth, however, any area of diminished current is a potential ambush point.

Current slows by bends in the river or creek. A good bass stream usually has several bends of various configurations where structure such as fallen trees and brush collects. Backwaters, or eddies, form behind submerged structure. Eddies attract largemouth and facilitate foraging activity. For this reason, bends produce well on most tributaries; they just seem to collect bass.

Bends also create a variance in the depth of the channel, which is conducive to big-bass habitation. The flow gouges out the bottom and outer bank, creating a deep, steep bank. Wooden debris piling up at these bends is often the only structure available.

Tributary Triumph

I recently fished a reservoir with little luck and decided to move to a tributary. The depth at the creek's entrance was a mere two feet, so I had to keep my bass rig on plane to cut across the blockage of heavy vegetation. Having enough momentum to break through the weed barrier was the key to discovering the great bass fishing on the other side.

Once beyond the clogged passageway, the five- to six-foot-deep creek waters meandered through lily pads toward the nearby forest. Soon, cypress and oak trees bordered the small stream and cast shadows over much of the water. In two short hours of midmorning fishing, I caught nine largemouth bass in some of the fastest fishing I've ever had. The bass ranged from 1 to about 4 pounds. The action never ceased.

I found two distinct patterns. First, the deep holes gouged out by heavy current were productive areas. The largemouth positioned themselves in the slower water below and to the side of the fast current.

The second prime location was on the submerged brush in the outer bends of the small stream. Those bends were deeper than the runs, and submerged tree limbs drew bass like magnets.

I attracted at least one largemouth from each similar area with short, 4- and 6-inch plastic worms, which I cast to a bluff bank and crawled back into the stream, dropping down where a bass was often waiting. While I caught no real lunkers, the average size of bass on the bends was impressive.

Shoreline Cover

Overhanging trees, fallen branches and submerged brush can offer river largemouth a shallow, protected home with plenty of food. Such terrain also provides excellent shade, which seems important for the bass in a shallow river system as opposed to those in a deep lake or reservoir.

The shoreline cover's relation to the sun should always be considered. The smart angler uses this in conjunction with the bank cover for best results. In winter I'll fish the sun-warmed shore first because it may be a degree or two warmer. Direct rays on that bank may also attract some forage out of hiding to bask in the sun.

Indentations in the shoreline may denote the presence of a feeder stream. Excellent structure in the form of a steep-sided underwater point is often created when a small stream or run-in converges with a river. Often a drop forms in this area that's worth several casts. Bass usually lie in the slower moving current near the confluence waiting for food.

Prime Targets

The exposed roots of a submerged tree adjacent to deeper water attract baitfish and bass. Casting to overhanging brush where bugs, grasshoppers, worms and other morsels periodically fall into the water is productive. Submerged timber creates an eddy on one side as water is channeled around the obstruction. Cast into this backwash where bass await their next meal.

Spring-fed waters produce a variety of bass, like the author's 2½-pound Suwannee bass. Even river largemouth find the crayfish an important part of their diet. A plug resembling the crustacean will produce!

Submerged logs provide cover for small minnows and bass. Cast parallel to and near the structure. Points jutting into the water and sloughs off a main channel are excellent targets for NAFC members to remember. In muddy or off-color water anglers can work the well-defined targets closer and fine-tune their casting and presentation. Smaller tributaries may be clearer after sustained high winds, so use small lures and light lines. They may be more roily after a thunderstorm, allowing use of larger gator-tail worms and baitcasting gear.

While stained water is easy to flip with a swinging, underhand cast, most of the successful river anglers use pinpoint casts of 15 to 25 feet. Naturally, on a creek barely wider than the boat, NAFC members should pick targets in front of them. Some of the smallest flows offer jig-and-worm tossers the best spring bass angling opportunities. Sandbars and shallow flats are prime spots to fish at this time.

Successful river angling requires the ability to read the unique topography, to determine an appropriate lure based on forage availability and current parameters and to present that bait correctly to the bass. Fishermen may have to make a challenging trek to discover the better opportunities. Most anglers overlook the river bass fishery, but you won't hear us river rats complain about the lack of competition.

Water Clarity

Some states are blessed with large deposits of limestone, which contribute to a network of underground and above-ground river systems. Calm, pristine waterways meander through pastures and swamps. Many are crystal clear, yet harbor multitudes of bass that have seldom seen a fisherman's lure.

Clear water generally isn't nutrient-rich. It does not afford a food base conducive to large bass growth. Under normal circumstances, maximum weights of 10 to 12 pounds are achievable for bass in spring-fed waters in the South. Stained water, depth and other influences contribute to maximum largemouth growth.

Calcareous waters (waters with suspended calcium carbonate) dictate a food chain somewhat unique to bass territories. Stomach content analysis by fishery biologists reveals that up to

Indentations are often inhabited by king-size bass. The small inlet out of the main current provides predators with a point for ambush. Smart NAFC members will cast to such spots.

90 percent of the food intake of stream bass can be crayfish. This factor helps an angler determine the appropriate lures and bait to use. Brown and red plastic worms are ideal, as are the many plastic crayfish imitations. Small spinners and spoons directly imitate the smaller fish forage on which the largemouth often feed.

Enterprising NAFC members can create their own bass catching spots. When running tributaries, position your boat near shore so that the wake stirs up the water adjacent to the shoreline. The disturbance also knocks small forage into the water. Bass will soon move along the area to feed. Then, turn the boat around and fish the banks with the stained water.

During the late spring when rivers are full and draining into lakes, the pH levels near the mouth of such tributaries often change drastically. Such areas are highly visible when the runoff is muddy and the lake is relatively clear. In general, late spring brings more fluctuation of pH levels, which can change every hour.

Fall brings the decay of fallen leaves and other plants, decreasing water clarity and pH levels. River fish move to shallower waters as their ideal pH range rises. When aquatic plants begin to go dormant for the winter, the pH level in creeks and tributaries will be affected first and start its downward trend.

13

Tidewaters

Bass fishermen often steer clear of brackish tributaries and streams. NAFC members are more likely to fish inland reservoirs, natural lakes and rivers. Few are aware that estuaries harbor waters with excellent, overlooked bass fishing.

Thousands of miles of tidal tributaries stretch along the Gulf coast around the Florida peninsula and up the Atlantic coast. The productivity of these brackish waters often surpasses that of inland waters. Estuaries teem with largemouth bass forage such as both fresh- and saltwater fingerlings, shrimp, crabs, snails and salamanders.

While hungry bass may be as numerous as their forage, an understanding of tidal influences is vital for angler success. Barometric pressure causes changes in water levels, which influence temperature and clarity. Tides dry up shoreline habitat during low periods as they sweep estuary forage along in their current.

Bass fishermen have long known that barometric pressure affects fishing, but few realize its impact on tidal action. Barometric pressure is established primarily by the moon's orbit. This pressure forces a large body of water downward in one area, creating a low tide. Elsewhere on the area's perimeter the water level rises slightly.

The moon orbits the earth in an elliptical path every 28 days. Its gravitational pull on the earth's seas is not uniform.

The sun also has some gravitational pull that affects the tides. These parameters, along with others, go into making the tide tables that you find in coastal areas.

Tide Timing

Without going into a lot of detail, tides can be categorized as either spring tides or neap tides. Both relate to the phases of the moon. Gravitational pull of the water is highest when the moon is closest to the earth and in line with the sun (spring tide). Spring tides occur every two weeks in most areas, during the new and full moon phases. Spring tides have the highest high tides and the lowest low tides. You see less rise and fall on a neap tide, which usually occurs on the first- and third-quarter moon phases. NAFC members should check the moon to determine the tidal phase the night before a fishing trip.

Tides repeat themselves about every 14 days. They occur approximately one hour later each day. Tide tables list the depths of the water at coastal locations as mean, or average, low tide. While the level can be lower, few anglers realize that the tide still flows after the lowest (or highest) point of the tide.

In tidal waters, correlating the tables from the reference station nearest your favorite fishing spots is extremely difficult. The tide delay depends on several factors such as depth, width, freshwater discharge, wind, rain and runoff. Observation is the best way to determine tide delay. Once you establish this time differential for a particular area, tides are predictable. The selection of optimum times to pursue bass can then be made from the tide tables days ahead of time.

Falling tides force baitfish from their hideouts into the main channel. Fast flowing water sweeps weaker swimmers toward their predators. This is why the falling tide is, in general, the most productive phase of tidal bass fishing. Rising tides open up shorelines and flats for fish to feed, resulting in some good fishing if one hits it right. The slow time in brackish water bass fishing is the time lapse between the change of tides.

After the lull during slack tide, bass proceed to feed on incoming tidal currents but with somewhat less vigor. At high tide when the marshy flats are flooded, topwater plugs, small spinners and weedless spoons occasionally entice feeders from the grass. Feeding activity again slows near high slack tide and

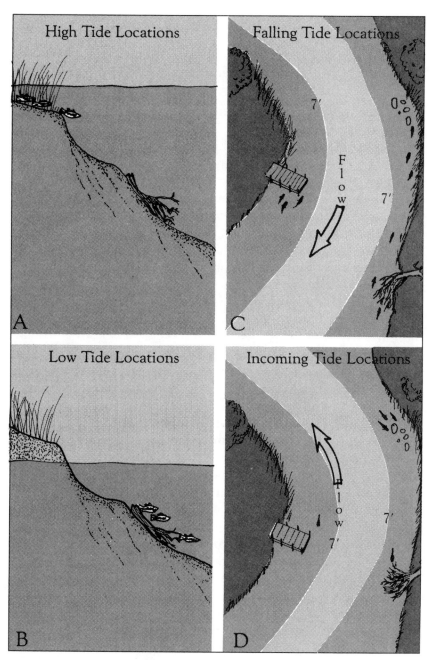

High Tide Locations

A

Falling Tide Locations

7'

0 °°°

F
l
o
w

7'

C

Low Tide Locations

B

Incoming Tide Locations

0 °°°

f
l
o
w

7'

7'

D

Understanding how rising or falling tides affect bass will help you target your fishing efforts. Falling tides are generally the most productive.

Tidewaters

generally remains slow until the tide falls rapidly.

Salty Considerations

Since a falling tide is generally better, most anglers launch their boats at dead high tide. Then they have about four or five hours of outgoing tide before a turnaround in flow and, many times, in bass activity.

Although current has the biggest influence on bass feeding activity day in and day out, wind, cold fronts and muddy water also alter the movements substantially. This is especially true during neap tide when water level changes are minimal. Strong winds can accelerate or even reverse tidal current flow. At these times, the feeding is unpredictable.

You seldom find deep-water structure in these waters. Very little submerged brush exists on the marsh flat areas of rivers and creeks, but the shallow marsh grass at the bank is thick and rugged. Creek bends in the wooded sections often contain brush piles near the bank, and fallen trees occasionally dot the shoreline in those areas.

Barnacles in brackish waters can be a problem. Break-offs are common when fishing near docks, piers or logs. Many tidal rivers and their tributaries contain submerged brush that is coated with the saltwater crustacean, so beware.

Both barnacles and crabs can give anglers fits while they are trying to worm their way to some good bass. Crabs often grab a plastic worm, fooling an angler into setting the hook. If a bass does grab the worm, it may wrap the line around a tree where the knife-like barnacles slice the line in two. One way to avoid such "salty" harassment is to fish a couple of miles up any freshwater creeks.

Floodwaters and severe changes in weather also lessen the certainty of a nice stringer of tidal bass. Heavy rains can lower the salinity of shallow brackish water and force fish toward the sea, while a drought or long period of dry weather can result in greater saltwater intrusion, moving the bass upstream. This depends a great deal on the flowage rates of the tributaries. As salinity increases, bass tolerance for brackish water wanes, so it's important to know the salt content of the water.

As the water freshens and becomes tolerable for acclimated bass, the plant life takes on a slightly different character.

By taking into account the effects rising and falling tides have on bass, you can focus your angling energies on the most productive areas and patterns.

Noting the presence of aquatic plants near the shoreline is one way of determining where the brackish water begins on a river. Lily pads and water hyacinths show up much more often in fresher water because both have low resistance to high salt content. Numerous arrowhead and elephant ear plants denote waters fresh enough for largemouth.

Prime Locations

Bass generally find the fresher waters. Cuts where shallow areas run into tidal rivers are prime spots. Baitfish congregate in these feeder streams, and bass are often there during an outgoing tide. The same tide leaves fallen weeds along the bank and mud flats. You often find largemouth on the quick drops just off the shallow flats. These give them a choice of depth or vegetation cover.

There are plenty of logs, stumps and eddy areas in most tidal rivers. But rivers change from one tide to the next. Outer bends may be consistent on either tide but the nature of the run just above and below it determines the current speed on each tidal phase. A sharp bend immediately in front of another bend slows

An undiscovered fishery exists in most tidal waters. Many giant largemouth swim brackish currents in search of shrimp, crabs and other unusual forage.

current action. A long, straight run allows it to move faster.

Tidal action in the tributaries varies from coast to coast. Brackish waters on the East Coast experience two high and two low tides each day, while tributaries on the Gulf side generally experience only one high and one low tide. The farther west NAFC members or other anglers go, the more difficult it is for them to detect any tidal action.

Once you establish a pattern and are catching bass, work these brackish waters hard—there are usually several fish in a given area. On several jaunts to a tidal bassin' hole my partner and I have often taken a dozen bass from a single creek bend.

Plastic worms, particularly the salt-impregnated kind, fool their share of bass in the tidal river bends. When the tide falls so much that shoreline structure lies exposed, largemouth bass will take floating balsa lures retrieved across the shallow flats. As the tide continues to fall, successful anglers switch back to worms to probe the river bends.

Southern Tidewaters

Florida's St. Johns River, near its entrance to the Atlantic ocean at Jacksonville, is covered with bass-filled piers and pilings. These structures are coated with saltwater crustaceans and barnacles. The docks attract big bass during the hot months. While my largest bass from these waters was just shy of 10 pounds, several over that mark are usually caught each month of the year in the area. All four major St. Johns' tributaries near its mouth are often overlooked as being saltwater. Yet they contain superb bass fishing.

River delta systems are more prevalent on the Gulf than along the Atlantic. The Apalachicola River is a good example of brackish water discharge into bays. The numerous bayous, sloughs and small hidden waterways just off Apalachicola Bay are full of largemouth bass. On a trip to that river I was casting worms in some of the muddiest water I've seen, with good results. After only two hours of fishing, I had seven largemouth. A 1-pound bluegill leaped on the surface ahead of our boat. I thought the small fish was forage in this instance and was probably being chased. Casting a three-inch topwater plug to the splash of the descending bluegill brought an immediate strike from a 7-pound, 10-ounce largemouth. It was a fine anchor for my stringer that day.

Most shallow tidal areas hold large numbers of bass. Those areas with numerous bends are better on the falling tide, while areas composed primarily of long runs between each bend are more productive on an incoming tide. Delta waters along the seaboard have substantial amounts of each.

Try fishing tidal waters. They harbor excellent, yet mostly overlooked, bass fishing.

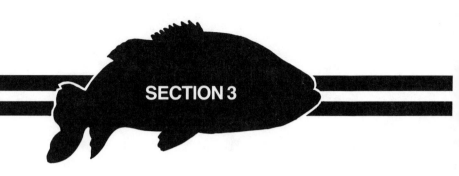

How To
Catch Bass

=====14=====

Crankbait Techniques

The productive crankbait fisherman keeps the plug hitting something. The speed at which you reel and the size of the lure are not as important. The plug must bounce off logs, weeds or the bottom a great deal of the time. So says Montgomery, Texas, bass guide and touring pro Rick Clunn.

Clunn is a long-time practitioner of diving plugs and a master at fishing them. He developed specific criteria upon which he bases his crankbait selection and technique. Clunn credits the crankbait with his first Classic win in 1976. He says it made his whole career, and he has done a lot with crankbaits since then.

"Crankbaits always play a role in my fishing," Clunn says. "You don't always end up catching all your fish on them in a tournament, but you learn a lot about the water when you practice with them. You may find hidden structure below the surface and then switch to a different lure to fish a spot more effectively."

For NAFC members, successful fishing rests on their ability to use time wisely. The crankbait not only catches bass but it helps you learn the water. Clunn firmly believes the bait allows an angler to find bass habitat that people throwing other lures will not discover.

People often don't get excited about fishing crankbaits until they see a full livewell. Then they get excited. A crankbait makes you work for fish, but no bait can cover water faster.

"It's not a fun bait," admits Clunn. "You can't go out there and expect vicious strikes, although occasionally one will almost knock the rod out of your hands. But you might catch doubles on it and there aren't many other lures that will do that."

Material Maneuvers

There are two types of crankbaits: wood baits and plastic baits. Selecting which to use depends on certain conditions.

Plastic baits, which can be fished slower, are usually associated with slightly colder water. This is because the fish's metabolism is slower and the best presentation is a slower retrieve.

Bass in cold waters relate more to the bottom and tend to be less aggressive, making plastic baits a good choice. When the water temperature drops to about 60 degrees, think about slowing the bait down. In warmer temperatures you can get away with a faster retrieve.

The advantage of fishing plastic baits slowly is that they don't have the natural buoyancy of wood. You can crank them down deep and then slow them down without having them rise toward the surface.

"When you slow down with wood baits," says Clunn, "they'll try to come back up off the bottom. Plastic baits tend to stay down and they have a wider wobble. In cold water I like my bait to wobble wider from side to side at slow speeds. Most wooden baits have much less vibration."

Plastic baits are ideal for fishing at night or in off-color water because the lure's side-to-side wobble displaces more water. Bass under those conditions seldom rely on their sight but depend more on their lateral line to find food. Clunn, who tosses crankbaits over 200 days each year, believes that plastic baits are a little easier for the bass to find under certain conditions.

"I like to use wooden baits in the warm-weather months when I'm fishing fairly fast," says Clunn. "In clearer waters I really burn a crankbait. When I reel the bait that fast I prefer the wood versions because they have very fine vibration. They move more like shad."

Rick Clunn believes in crankbaits not only for catching fish but for locating hidden structure.

Crankbait Techniques

Crankbait Benefits

The crankbait is probably the most versatile lure. Due to the different bills and sizes, you can work depths efficiently from one foot down to about 22. It can be used in almost any body of water and in a variety of bass habitats.

Base the selection of crankbait size upon several things, the most obvious being the available food supply at that time of year. If there are lots of small fry around in the late spring and early summer, then use smaller crankbaits. In the fall and winter when everything has matured, go to larger baits.

If there is a length limit on the waters you're fishing, you'll probably throw a bigger bait most of the time. So if you're trying to catch bigger fish—and I believe in the old adage that big baits catch bigger fish—then fish a bigger bait. If you are just trying to get a limit, go to smaller crankbaits that attract bass of all sizes.

The water color may also affect what size lure you go with. In murky or off-color water, fatter plastic baits, which displace more water, may be the better choice. In extremely clear water, a fast-moving bait in natural colors is usually more productive.

Bill shape and length are often more critical than body size. The bill controls the depth of the lure, and its size usually determines whether or not you can get deep enough to ricochet off available cover.

"If I'm fishing a 45-degree bank with stumps and rocks on it, then I use a deep-diving bait," states Clunn. "I cast it to the shallows and dig it until the lure moves on down and stays on the bottom for a long time. If I'm fishing heavy, shallow cover, say two to three feet, I don't need a deep-diving bait. I can get deep enough by bouncing a shallow runner through the stuff and seldom get hung up.

"The crankbait is just a tool," states Clunn, "and you have to learn the appropriate size of bill needed for the tool to cover the depth of water you want to fish."

Fishing And Flexing Factors

The rod is also extremely critical in crankbait fishing, according to Clunn.

"Many people won't throw crankbaits for long because they get too tired," says Clunn. "I used to fish them on a conventional 5½-foot rod and they wore me out. I was trying to fight that bait all day long with just my wrist.

"The crankbait is a fast-moving bait, and I feel it should be fished with a glass or glass-tip type rod," he says. "A fish moves on the fast-moving bait and tries to inhale it. Something has got to give it to him. A glass rod allows the fish to get it a little better than the high reflex-recovery, high-tech rods.

"You don't have to determine strikes on a crankbait. That's the key to the productivity of the glass rods," he explains. "The high-tech rods work to your disadvantage there too. Not only do they have fast flex recovery but you're working a fast bait and you react faster when you feel the strike. All of that results in poorly hooked fish. When a crankbait is moving fast and you have your hooks right, the fish hooks itself.

"Only on a worm-type bait do you want to feel the fish inhaling the bait," Clunn says. "With a crankbait, I want to be behind the fish. I want the rod to flex and give the bait to him. I don't even want to set the hook until he's closed on the bait. The response feels more sluggish, and that's contrary to what our modern minds think is right."

Distance And Depth Dependence

"The smartest thing I ever did was to go to a long-handled, 7-foot rod that I can brace against my wrist and against my side," says Clunn. "When throwing a crankbait I can use two hands and really put the bait out there a long way. Distance is not necessary with most bass fishing, but I think long casts are usually necessary when fishing crankbaits."

Clunn explains, "Crankbaits come back in a parabolic-type curve and reach their maximum depth at the bottom of the curve. Then the baits start coming back up at the boat. The longer you can keep a crankbait at its maximum depth, the more contact your bait will usually make and you'll catch more fish."

On short casts, crankbaits don't stay down as long, so their coverage at maximum depth is minimal. The long cast is beneficial in crankbait fishing, and the long rod helps you cast the lure farther.

How you hold the rod also influences how deep a crankbait runs. If you put the rodtip down below the surface of the water,

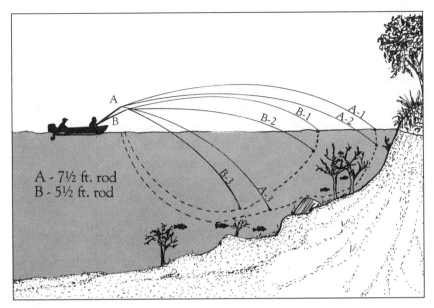

The advantages of a 7-foot rod (A) versus that of a 5½-footer (B) are further casting distance and a deeper lure trajectory (providing more time in the productive strike zone). The crankbait on the two rods are shown at lure touchdown (1), after four turns of the reel handle (2), and halfway into the retrieve (3).

the bait will descend deeper. Most cranking experts try to cast their lures as far as they can, usually about 40 yards, and retrieve with the tip down.

The line also controls the depth of the lure. Clunn doesn't often vary the line size. Although he occasionally goes to heavier line, he normally fishes 15-pound test. Rather than drop down in line size to get a bait to run deeper, he uses a bigger bill to achieve that goal. Knowing the depths at which your baits will run on a certain pound test is essential to fishing success.

The only time to drop to lighter line is in clear water when you want to get the bait to maximum depth. The crankbait normally digs into underwater structures. With 10-pound monofilament you lose more baits or waste more time going after them. With heavier line you have a better chance of pulling them loose.

"A crankbait is one of the least-fished baits," says Clunn. "Fish relate to angling pressure. If everyone is throwing a spinnerbait along a weedline, I may go to a small crankbait, even though it might be spinnerbait-type water. Changing the lure the fish sees may make a big difference."

Cast And Crank Variations

Bass may not see many crankbaits nor do they see many other baits at typical crankbait depths. Most anglers fish a worm right on the bottom and work plugs or spinnerbaits near the surface. Those areas receive the most pressure. The in-between zones are pretty much neglected.

Most of the strikes come when the crankbait is hitting something. That usually occurs at the deepest portion of the crankbait's descent. The second most common place to get a strike is right at the boat as the bait comes off the bottom and heads to the surface. Anglers should also be very conscious of what they're doing with the trolling motor when the bait is nearing the boat. At that point you should expect a strike.

"Trolling motors are getting more and more powerful," says Clunn, "and we tend to emphasize move, move, move. The minute my bait approaches the boat, I turn off the motor switch and give the fish an opportunity to hit."

Clunn rarely varies his retrieve. Most of the time he lets the objects vary the retrieve. Occasionally he consciously stops the lure, especially when fishing during the colder months or if casting to a spot where he has pinpointed bass.

"I depend mostly on deflection of the bait for strikes, and that comes from hitting stuff," says Clunn. "The second best technique for me is the stop-and-go retrieve. I just reel it very fast, stop and hold it."

"Normally I find that fish want this presentation when my bait is stopped by a limb and doesn't deflect over it," he says. "One or two strikes in this instance tell me something. I then intentionally use the stop-and-go retrieve each time the bait ticks something. That's just being observant and paying attention to what the fish are trying to tell you."

Design Variations For Productivity

Good crankbait fishermen lose baits. NAFC members need to run the bait into logs and brush to get the majority of nonaggressive bass. If you get the bait to deflect off the structure, you double your chance of getting a fish.

Crankbaits are most effective when hitting tree limbs, rock walls or even the lake bottom. You'll lose plenty of baits if you intentionally run them into objects, but you'll catch more bass.

In order to keep the bait in contact with either the structure or the bottom, you have to get it to descend to the appropriate depth. That is a problem for some anglers, according to most lure designers.

"A lot of people think that the harder you crank a diving plug, the deeper it'll go," says lure designer Lee Sisson. "The truth is that you can actually over-crank a crankbait, and it's not only unloading off to the side of the lip but off the front, too. That drives the bait back up instead of letting it achieve its maximum depth. Most of the baits I experiment with achieve their maximum depth at a moderate speed."

You can generally over-crank a shallow-running bait because there is not as much surface area on its smaller lip. A plug with a long, slender lip would be more difficult to over-crank than one with a big, rounded lip. The latter automatically goes deeper.

The water flowing over the lip itself causes a buildup of resistance as the bait slices through the water. That's why all crankbaits pull back. After a certain amount of resistance builds up it has to unload somehow. It starts vibrating, dumping off on one side and then the other. That begins the vibration pattern.

"A lot of people don't realize that the lip is just part of the diving plane," explains Sisson. "That's why you can't take a giant lip and put it on a little bait. You must have something for that lip to work against. The back of the lure itself becomes part of the diving plane. A fatter bait has more surface for the lip to work against and it will go deeper. A longer bait has similar characteristics."

Some baits are designed to get down deep, yet have a small silhouette, somewhere between the injured-minnow type and the fat, diving style. The surface area on the back of such lures has to be properly designed for the bait to get down into the snags. The added area also means more buoyancy to help the lure float up from hang-ups.

Snags and Depths

NAFC members know that hang-ups can be a problem, but relatively few of us lose more than two or three baits on snags

Match the shape and color of your crankbaits to the predominant forage to help you catch more bass. Silver- or white-sided baits resemble threadfin shad.

during a full day of fishing. Improved versions of "plug knockers" (lure retrievers) and heavy line account for the relatively low number. The latter is the key.

A good procedure to follow when snagged is to "pop" the line by grabbing it with your hand, stretching it and then quickly letting it go. If the recoil doesn't work, steadily pull it with the rodtip pointed at the snag to a point just before the breaking strength. Most of the time, one of these methods will free the plug. The third and final solution is to go after it.

A lure has less chance of getting hung up and reaches its maximum depth if it's tuned properly and running straight. Most untuned lures I have observed run to one side or the other, not straight ahead. That's not to say that a lure that runs off to one side won't catch fish. Sometimes that's what the fish are looking for.

NAFC members who are serious about bass fishing should take their baits to a swimming pool or to any place with clear water where they can watch them run. You need to make sure that the lures are doing what they are supposed to do.

Because of the lure's pull many people believe it's going 18 feet deep. But some are just hard-pulling lures and may run only a few feet down.

The reason is simple. When you pull any lure down, you are pulling a bunch of line down too. The line doesn't go straight from the rodtip to the lure. The line makes a big bow and goes almost straight down near the bait. The heavier the line, the more resistance.

Shake, Rattle And Roll

"The vibration pattern of a crankbait is what attracts bass," states Sisson. "I think there are several factors that cause a fish to strike. I call them strike stimuli. They feel the vibration pattern a long time before they ever see it. That pattern either turns them on or off. They may watch the bait go by, swim away from it or be stimulated enough by it to move in for a closer look. -

"Built-in rattles and sound chambers only add to the vibration pattern because sound is just vibration whether it is moving through air or water," explains Sisson. "Shad, crayfish, shrimp and most baitfish make a high-pitched sound. Fishery biologists have described the sound as similar to the noise given off when two rocks are tapped together underwater."

Any movement through water puts out a vibration pattern. You can pull a piece of line through water to verify this. Some people think light line is best to fish with a crankbait because the lure will work better and dive deeper. Sisson agrees, but he also notes that light line moves less water and thus makes less noise.

"The next stimulus is what I call flash patterns," Sisson says. "These attract the eye of the bass before it really sees the lure. They're the first visual contact the fish has with a bait that is moving through the water and throwing off flashes."

Paints have been developed that give off a flash pattern in different colors. Silver or gold are popular, but many crankbait manufacturers now use red and blue. Chromes and some bright colors like chartreuse seem to give off a glow around the lure.

"The next strike stimulus is the body size and shape of the lure," Sisson says. "What the bass sees when it gets there is important. Does the bait really look like something to eat?"

Resemblance to the existing forage is just one of the strike stimuli, but it's important in the overall picture when enticing the fish to take the lure. Silhouette size is a consideration throughout the seasons. In the spring, bass will eat little minnows, and in the fall they gorge themselves on bigger forage.

Material Witness

Every material has advantages and disadvantages. Plastic lures are generally easier to manufacture in large numbers. There are some excellent plastic baits on the market. You can usually abuse them a little more than you can a balsa wood lure.

One of their chief limitations, according to Sisson, is that their density is heavier than water. Air cavities must be built into the plastic lures, and building extremely small ones without forfeiting strength or buoyancy can be a problem.

"Balsa wood is not as tough, but it is light. Its density is less than that of water, so you have to add weight to it to get it to do what you want," says Sisson. "You must add strength to a soft foundation through wire harnesses and epoxy glues. Its flotation is an advantage, and you can put weight where you want it. Balsa is a soft wood that is easily worked."

Balsa wood baits are not as strong as plastic baits but are light enough to cast into shallow areas without spooking fish.

Foam lures are a lot like balsa in flotation characteristics, according to Sisson. He believes that they are less expensive to manufacture than plastic baits. In making a foam lure, the critical element is metering the foam to get the right amount in the mold.

"A hardwood is midway between a plastic and a balsa in durability and strength," points out Sisson. "It has a strong foundation, but its density is lighter than water. You don't have to build strength into it like you do balsa. A lure with controlled weight placement is one that normally runs easier.

Rattles in baits that add to the vibration were initially an accident, as Sisson tells it. A plastic bait manufacturer was putting weights in his lures and accidentally put small weights (designed for a smaller plug) in a large plug. The manufacturing defect caused a rattling sound. It also caused a craze! Many good things in this business start off as accidents.

The Final Components

Keep crankbait hooks razor-sharp. You can over-sharpen them only if you make them so thin that the point bends over on the first object you hit. Wise anglers constantly check the sharpness when pulling on the bait, getting it hung and digging it through stuff. When on the water, be ready to change to a fresh set of hooks. Replace old hooks on your baits prior to going out on the water.

Rebend a straightened hook only if you are fishing open water. If you are in heavy cover and are having to exert a lot of pressure to horse the fish from the habitat, never reform the hook to its normal shape. Replace the crankbait. If you have to straighten the hooks repeatedly, it may be best to change them.

Every component of a lure plays a part in eliciting strikes. Design or manufacturer inconsistencies in any one of them can ruin a plug's performance.

The eye where the split ring is attached is the key to tuning a lure. Bend it in the direction you want the lure to run. A lure can be tuned to run to one side, to bounce around each post in a row or to run under a pier. That can be particularly advantageous in the summer when bass are holding tighter to pilings. The result is a lure that resembles a crayfish trying to get on a log.

The depth a lure runs can be adjusted by making it run sideways. If a lure running true normally attains eight feet, it can be tuned to run to one side and possibly only get down to four feet. Such a method is productive in shallow water as long as the lure doesn't achieve what the designers call "critical roll," where the bait will go into a spin.

Fishing a crankbait effectively is often a lot more complicated than just casting and reeling in areas holding fish. These tips will help you take more fish—if you try them.

15

Worming Techniques

The water couldn't have been more than four feet deep at the edge of the rushes where Wayne Yohn had just manhandled a 10-pound largemouth into the boat. The boat's dash-mounted flasher was full of red blips denoting weeds from the surface on down.

That fish was nothing for the bass guide to get excited about. He's caught more than 60 over the 10-pound mark.

Flippin' worms to the shallow "buggy whips" is Yohn's forte. Those bullrush clusters surrounded by huge beds of thinner grass vegetation are most productive for the Lakeland, Florida, resident. He proved it that day by capturing lunkers of 6½ and 10 pounds. After several photos, the veteran reed flipper returned both fish to the water.

"Fish both sides of a clump of reeds when flippin' worms," Yohn advises. "I've often fished one side without success and then picked up the bait and dropped it on the other side where a bass was waiting."

"Always watch the line," he continued, "because the slightest twitch may mean a strike. If that bush shakes when the lure falls to the bottom, chances are that the bass has it, and you can go ahead and set the hook.

"Bass seldom hit a worm on the fall during the spring, though," says the flippin' expert. "They are not actively feeding, so they'll strike the worm as you move it. If the bait drops too fast it can easily spook them, so lighten up on the sinker. There are even times when $\frac{1}{16}$ ounce of lead is enough."

Yohn's yo-yo-type cast in shallow water is, by necessity, smooth and quiet. He raises the rodtip with the plastic worm just off the water's surface, strips off more line with his left hand and, with an underhand motion, swings the lure like a pendulum toward the weed clump. His left hand keeps some drag on the line and slows the lure's descent, allowing it to contact the surface noiselessly.

"Most of your worm fishing in these thickets is usually with less than 12 feet of line out," says Yohn. "Line control may be the most important key to successful flippin' for anglers just learning this technique."

Jungle Flippin'

In shallow, heavy cover such as bullrushes, Johnson grass or cattails, Yohn believes strongly in having adequate tackle for the job. His arsenal consists of an 8-foot, heavy-action flippin' rod and a spinning reel spooled with 30-pound-test monofilament. He catches numerous bass using 8-inch black grape worms adorned with a 5/0 worm hook and $\frac{5}{8}$-ounce slip sinker.

The most productive flippin' pattern during the entire spring period involves working the small bullrush clumps isolated within the emergent grass that abounds in shallow waters. Bigger bass are usually found shallow at this time. The action during the summer moves to dense buggy-whip patches or grassbeds in four or five feet of water. Again, movement in the weeds indicates fish.

The productive flipper moves in tight on points and pockets and checks the water depth and type of bottom. Bass prefer a clean, sandy bottom. Bullrushes are good prospective bass cover because they grow in sandy areas.

Yohn has utilized his bullrush worm-flippin' method to achieve great success in tournaments during the past several years. In a one-day tournament, Yohn and a partner amassed a 60-pound, 2-ounce, flippin'-caught stringer of bass to outfish 142 competitors. Yohn himself pulled in two largemouth more than 10 pounds, a 7-pounder and several smaller fish from the rushes.

This Florida bass guide takes tons of huge bass each year flippin' worms to shallow stands of bullrushes. Notice his 8-foot, heavy-action rod.

Worming Techniques

Shallow Terrain

Most experienced shallow-water worm anglers prefer to flip a bait into bullrushes rather than cattail cover. Rushes are easier to fish because they are straight and rigid. Cattails, on the other hand, grow in shallower water and their leaves branch off as the plant rises from the water's surface. Both provide great shallow-water cover.

Reeds and cattails that grow in the better areas are taller due to optimal soil conditions. A good sandy soil is fertile, enhancing vegetation growth. Bass prefer that additional weed cover protection.

Flippin' is extremely effective in some situations. But it is only one of many successful plastic worm techniques applicable to the shallows. Emergent vegetation is usually prominent in shallow waters making them highly oxygen-enriched and forage-intensive. Many types of aquatic vegetation provide a source of food for predator and prey alike throughout all but the coldest months.

Shallow waters warm faster and "turn on" quicker with the first hint of spring. Hard bottoms are what attract bedding bass then. Shallows with adequate cover are accessible to most worm-tossing anglers, too. Even in the thicker, summer mass of milfoil, coontail and hydrilla, the plastics have a place.

The better worming areas are generally where a breakline or change occurs. This might be in the form of a weed-type variance, such as pickerelweed to cattails, or in a small depth change. Bass hold on a 12-inch drop or at the edge between two types of plants. The topography probably dictates the choice of worm rig.

A Texas-rigged worm produces well in shallows that have fairly clean bottoms and vegetation that is rigid and straight. The rig with a 3/0 or 4/0 worm hook turned back into itself to make it weedless, and a bullet-shaped slip sinker on the line in front is the most popular of all. It is probably also the most versatile.

The sliding weight should be as light as possible in the shallows, particularly around heavy masses of vegetation. A 1/16- or 1/8-ounce sinker is ideal for most shallow weed infestations. Casting bulky worms keeps the fare out of bottom cover and in the strike zone.

Maximizing the catch from certain weed masses in the shallows may require the use of different rigs and presentations. Several surface or near-surface worm rigs may be more effective. The primary idea is to make the plastic bait appear like a snake swimming through the cover.

Swimming Attractors

Submergent vegetation that grows from the bottom toward the surface may have a water shelf just above it. Just a foot or two between the surface and the weedbed is sufficient to work either a swimming worm or floating worm rig across a shallow expanse without fear of getting entangled. Both rigs sport exposed hooks that make them less appropriate for other shallow-water habitat.

The swimming worm rig has been deadly in protected waters among vegetation beds and along defined banks for about 20 years. The kinky-shaped rig utilizes a No. 1 straight-shank hook threaded a third of the way into the head of a straight-tail worm. Only the hook's barb protrudes, leaving the worm with a bend in it. A black swivel is tied about 12 inches in front of the worm to prevent line twist as the lure twirls through the water.

Purple with a glo-pink tail is a hard color combination to beat. The swivel, hook and 6-inch worm provide the only weight for casting purposes. This is sufficient for the spinning gear to achieve a steady retrieve back to the boat. Small canal and pond bass especially favor this rig. The exposed hook allows for an easy hookset and the weightlessness entices the bass to hold onto the lure longer.

I first used this rig on an ultra-light outfit along a mile-long canal. The bottom sloped gradually from the bank past sparse aquatic weeds to a depth of only five feet or so. Most of the 15 largemouth that I caught and released were in about two feet of water, waiting for a slow-moving morsel.

Floating And Belly-Hooked Models

The floating worm rig encompasses a highly buoyant worm along with a light, gold-plated wire hook in a 2/0 or 3/0 size. A long, 8- to 10-inch fat body worm with a paddle tail provides optimum flotation. The hook, positioned one-third of the way down the worm's body, is lightweight, allowing the rig to be twitched along the surface over grassbeds in slow jerks.

Snake the rig slowly across the surface and stop it periodically so it lies motionless. When fishing extremely heavy cover, embed the hook in the worm Texas-style. Add a foam snake head to the rig to help its flotation. It's easy to see the strike on this rig in most situations and that's exciting. A surface explosion will long be remembered.

Another rig that draws a lot of attention from largemouth inhabiting hydrilla and milfoil expanses is a belly-hooked worm. Simply fish the 6-inch straight worm with the exposed 3/0 hook through the midsection sans weight.

When fishing any of the worm rigs described, shallow-water anglers should keep their rodtips high. You can more easily see and feel the hits. Slack can be quickly given if needed.

A weedless worm rig that sinks into pockets in the vegetation will be an effective one. With most shallow worm rigs you can slow the bait considerably to entice a "follower" or one of the more deliberate lunkers that swim shallow, weed-infested waters.

As soon as shallow water temperatures warm to 55 degrees there's a worm rig that will produce. Most of the possibilities are exciting to fish. What's better, they catch bass.

Slow And Fast Ways To Lure Bass

Bass are finicky eaters during their spawning activities, so pay careful attention to fishing techniques, particularly the speed of retrieve, to be successful. At other times of the year a lightning fast retrieve may be necessary for maximum action. "Dead worming" is one technique that was developed and refined for use during an eight-week period in the spring. The secret of a few productive anglers for many years, the dead worm method may be the best way to entice a spawning or post-spawn bass to strike. It takes a lot of patience and finesse.

Fishing a dead worm requires an angler to remain alert, with fingers sensitive to the lightest pickup. Springtime bass on the bed, or just coming off it, seldom spend energy to charge the plastic bait. They mouth the bait gently as they pick it up. The angler must feel that movement through the rod.

Most anglers experience occasional soft-tap action with the more conventional worm fishing techniques. The dead worm-

Belly-hooking a high-buoyant worm is productive when worked slowly on the surface. The strikes are explosive!

Worming Techniques

ing technique motivates spring bass to act. Coupled with a salt-impregnated worm, the system is the key to ending the short-strike syndrome exhibited by bedding and post-spawn largemouth. It's a difficult method to master, but deadly.

To fish plastic worms successfully using the dead worm technique, anglers must become line watchers. They must discriminate between a soft touch by an 8-pound bass and the bumping or nudging of underwater structure. The plastic lure should drop freely on a semi-taut line, slowly gliding downward rather than plummeting.

Careful observation of the line helps you detect any twitch or sideways movement. The line should be slack once the worm reaches the bottom. Let the worm settle to the bottom and rest there for at least 30 seconds.

Then, very slowly lower the rod and take in most of the slack while leaving a slight bow in the line. This allows you to see any critical movement without the bass getting suspicious. The rodtip should point about 60 degrees above the water's surface and directly in front of you for best detection of any resistance.

Retrieve Reasoning

Nothing is more important in successful dead worming than the retrieve. If you don't concentrate on the proper slow speed and depth control of the bait, you might as well forget it. Spring bass are exhausted after the spawning ordeal. They move very slowly and so must your bait.

With this technique at this time of year, it is very easy to fish too fast. You must inch the worm along with a series of light pulls and pauses.

Don't drop the bait off any underwater structure. During the retrieve, pause for at least five seconds and let the worm sit. A s-l-o-w retrieve is the key.

Observe the line and feel the bass habitat as you slowly work the bait through vegetation and other bottom structure. It's a waiting game, but dead wormin' takes spring bass. Bass are particularly curious in the spring. A largemouth must have plenty of time to inspect the offering and move into position to react to it.

On a clear spring day several years ago I found this

technique to be most effective. The canal on which I slowly floated had numerous beds along its bank. On my first cast to the shore, my worm landed on the grassy bank. I crawled the bait into the shallows and immediately saw a boil.

I quickly set the hook. A 7-pound, spawning female erupted on the surface trying to spit out the morsel that fooled her.

Even in the spring when bass concentrate their energy on bedding, they don't give up without a fight. I struggled to force her out of a nearby submerged tree and into the net. Always in favor of conservation, particularly at this time of the year, I gained further satisfaction by releasing the trophy.

Canal Bank Variation

I find that shallow canals off deep water are often loaded with bass. I use a fairly successful technique involving a variation of the dead worm (rigged self-weedless) to catch these canal fish. The technique is most effective using a salt-impregnated worm.

Again, the slow speed of the worm action is the key. After casting it up on the bank, allow the plastic bait to sit for a minute or more without letting the line hit the water's surface.

Then, slowly crawl the scented wiggler into the water where the weight of the hook lets it fall. The worm should sit still in six to 12 inches of water at the canal bank for at least half a minute. Bass often approach and inhale the worm.

On one fishing trip to a nearby canal, I caught and released more than 20 bass weighing over 5 pounds each using this unique approach. I find fishing this technique during the spawning period most consistent and successful.

Rigging For Slow Going

I prefer to dead worm with a Texas-style rig and a 4/0 worm hook anchored with a ⅛- or ¹⁄₁₆-ounce bullet sinker. Line testing 14 to 17 pounds allows for better buoyancy and water drag than lighter lines. It also provides a softer approach to an observant bass.

Decrease line size when fishing areas with little cover in clear water or for bass weighing less than 7 or 8 pounds. Whatever the line, however, keep in mind that the slower a worm descends to the bottom, the better the chances of a bass

The "streaking worm" retrieve produces on occasion when "normal" retrieve fails to interest fish. Larsen likes to streak worms on windy days.

mouthing it. Similarly, the slower it crawls on the bottom, the better the chances of a strike. Sharp hooks are equally vital to angler success.

Figuring out bedding and post-spawn bass is not easy. They are easier to catch in a pre-spawn period. Individual clean-sand bass beds on flats indicate the beginning of the season. Other sure signs of spawning bass are a pH approaching 7.4, water temperature readings in the mid 60s and numerous big bass that will not strike.

Bass experiencing the spring doldrums can be motivated by dead worming. Patient NAFC members will soon find results on their line. Even so, releasing any fish caught is the best mode of operation during this time of year.

Suspending Or Streaking

A strike on extremely slow- or fast-moving worm rigs can occur any time, even next to the boat. The "suspended" worm is another slow version that you gently twitch along through heavy emergent cover or just under floating cover such as duckweed. A 3/0 or 4/0 Tru-Turn Brute hook turned into an 8-inch worm is light enough to make the rig neutrally buoyant. No weight is added.

In sparse vegetation the hook point can be left exposed without too much fear of entanglement. Work the rig from just below the surface down toward the bottom, depending on how you retrieve it. Strikes on the slow wiggling bait will usually be premeditated and, in shallow water, observable.

A friend and I first tried the "streaking worm" retrieve several years ago in gale-force winds. A shallow point in the small reservoir sported whitecaps—and bass. We initially had a largemouth slam a Texas-rigged worm as it was being quickly reeled (buzzed) to the boat. A few minutes later, that happened again. We began using the quick retrieve on each cast.

We eventually took off the bullet weight because we didn't need the extra weight to cast 40 yards with the wind. We used worms that were 8 and 9 inches in length, ideal for casting without a sinker and great for attracting attention as they made their way across a choppy surface. The 18 or so bass that exploded on the fast-retrieved offerings were chunky, up to 7 pounds.

I often use the streaking worm method over windy shallows, and it remains effective. It's particularly productive over submergent vegetation that does not encroach upon the surface. A 4/0 or 5/0 worm hook handles most strikes. A slight pause before the hookset is generally advantageous. Setting the hook too quickly results in lost fish. Largemouth on a shallow, wind-blown bar or point are active, feeding fish, so the strikes are always exciting.

Slow Night Action

Don't put away the plastic wigglers when the sun goes down. Bass move en masse to the shallows after dark to feed, and most anglers would be surprised at the worm action available then.

Some tips may help. Darker hues of plastic, such as black, purple or blue-grape, offer more distinct silhouettes, help the bass home in on the target. Fatter worms fished on the surface present more bulk and thus are of more interest to the larger predators below.

If you can get away with a faster retrieve, imitation snakes and eels offer maximum tail action. Paddle tails and curlytail worms and eels send off vibrations only if moved. Slow, steady retrieves usually offer maximum action. The fare is easier for the bass to find.

Use short casts and stay alert. Control, observation and feel will be enhanced, resulting in fewer strikes missed. Bullet-shaped rattle floats and weights, light-stick additives and glowing plastics are the latest wrinkle in night worming, and they do produce.

Try some slow retrieves or lightning fast ones to increase results. Fast rigs are fun and sometimes productive. Slow ones are usually more successful, but not always. Keep both retrieves in mind next time you're on the water.

16

Spinnerbait Tactics

The spinnerbait never really gained respect until Ken Cook, a fisheries-biologist-turned-professional-angler from Elgin, Oklahoma, used one to win $100,000 in a 1983 bass tournament. He tossed a 24-karat Gold Eagle spinnerbait to amass more than 41 pounds of bass in the four-day event.

Cook and 258 other professional anglers battled a March cold front with unseasonable winds gusting to 50 miles per hour and cold water temperatures in their quest for the giant jackpot. Cook was one of only a few who caught fish each day. Since then the spinnerbait has received a lot more recognition and respect.

Cook has caught many bass since on the same bait. He relies on modifications during tough times. In one tournament he located bass in thick, brushy treetops in 10 to 15 feet of water. The fish were holding six feet deep in the thickest tangles.

Cook modified the heavy Gold Eagle (½-ounce) spinnerbait by replacing the standard No. 6 blade with a smaller No. 4 Colorado blade. This allowed the lure to fall easier and faster into the thick limb cover, making for a more efficient presentation. Most bass hit the lure after it fell off a limb.

"I further enhanced the vibration produced by the blade by flattening it out somewhat with a pair of pliers," says Cook. "A flatter blade vibrates more than a deeply cupped blade of similar size. This gave a hard vibration that attracted bass better without producing excessive water resistance, which would keep the bait from falling as quickly."

Cook won that tournament with 15 bass that weighed a total of 45 pounds, 13 ounces.

The state of the art regarding spinnerbaits has progressed more rapidly than many other lure technologies. NAFC members toss spinnerbaits bearing swivels attached to blades of various sizes. Some are size- and shape-adjustable. Some have a rotating blade nearest the head. Others have thin wire shafts that enhance the spinner vibrations. Some even have an upper shaft that pivots back out of the way of a strike. And the innovations have not been exhausted yet.

Speed Considerations

NAFC members today count on the spinnerbait in many situations. It is effective and easy to handle under most conditions. Best of all, it is a fast bait that can quickly eliminate water and find fish, a characteristic valued by pros like Cook and Rick Clunn. Clunn has caught some of his biggest bass on spinnerbaits. In fact, the professional angler fishes with spinnerbaits whenever he's after a big fish.

"I used Stanley's ½-ounce spinnerbait with a transparent skirt at Lake Meade in a major bass contest," said Clunn. "The head design allows it to come through the thickest cover. That's where you normally want to throw a spinnerbait. It should be making contact with the cover."

That lure was responsible for his impressive victory. He combined its use with a technique that he has utilized for many years in clear, warm water. The spinnerbait can be ripped at maximum speed for maximum production under such circumstances. It won't roll or turn over on its side, either, according to Clunn.

In the old days, spinnerbaits were built differently. In one tournament, he even added a ½-ounce rubber-core sinker to the spinnerbait. That very effective rig helped to keel the bait during a fast retrieve.

He ripped the bait across the surface of the water over huge beds of milfoil. The bass waited until the spinnerbait got halfway back to the boat, and then they slammed it. He caught

The spinnerbait is effective and easy to fish in most situations. Best of all, it's a fast bait that can be used to quickly eliminate unproductive waters.

Spinnerbait Tactics

several bass in the 4-, 5- and 6-pound range that day and won a major bass championship.

Clunn used the extra weight trick for many years and still does when necessary. Often, he takes a ½-ounce spinnerbait and adds another ¼- to ½-ounce rubber-core sinker to the blade shaft.

Size Considerations

Most anglers naturally have their own ideas regarding the best spinnerbait size to use. The proper selection depends on what the angler is trying to accomplish, typical size of fish, water conditions and so forth. Spinnerbaits come in a variety of sizes. There should be one in your tackle box that's appropriate for every condition.

The size of the forage the fish are feeding on and, to some extent, the average size of bass present in the water being fished dictate the size of lure. Try to determine that, regardless of how difficult it may be.

"In clear water conditions I would probably go with a ⅛-ounce spinnerbait," Clunn says. "Where bass grow bigger I use a bigger spinnerbait with larger blades. On other waters that are full of small bass, I might even use the bigger bait.

"There are millions of undersized bass in some waters," explains Clunn, "and I would probably go to a little larger spinnerbait to discourage some of the little fish. Culling by increasing the size of the lure should be an option."

Shaft And Blade Selections

Thin spinnerbait shafts are now in vogue. Many feel they produce more strikes. The main problem with them, however, is that they are not as durable as some made with larger diameter wire. A spinnerbait that has caught 10 or 15 fish has done more than most lures ever will. Thin-shaft spinnerbaits are prone to breakage after that number of fish. Knowledgeable anglers don't take a chance on it. They use a new one.

Big blades cause more wear on thin shafts than do smaller blades. The wire on some spinnerbaits is tapered down to the blades. That makes them a little more durable than those with constant-diameter thin wire.

A blade running on a thinner wire shaft has more freedom

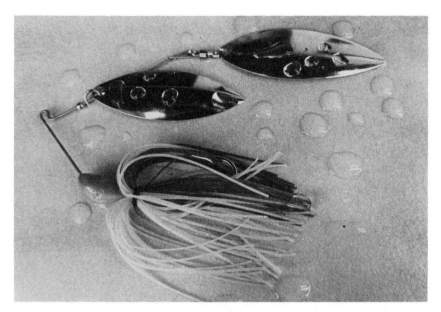

The flash and vibration pattern of a spinnerbait depends on the size and shape of the blades used. Switch often until you find the right combination.

than one off a thicker-shafted bait. More vibrations are possible at slow speeds with large blades on thinner shafts. Even at faster speeds they perform well. Clunn prefers a tandem-bladed lure constructed with a small silver blade in front and a small willow leaf on the back.

Skirt Selections

The spinnerbait is a great tool, and with the number of skirt colors available, it has more flexibility than it has ever had. The skirts, originally designed for jigs, allow the angler to use a wide variety of metal flake colors. Clunn normally fishes white and chartreuse spinnerbaits but goes to other colors when conditions dictate a change.

Trailer Thoughts

Trailer or stinger hooks are not given a lot of thought until a big bass escapes a spinnerbait without one. They often pay for themselves with just one extra fish.

The conditions of the water and the habitat being fished should dictate whether or not you use a trailer hook. If the addition of a trailer hook increases the number of snags or hang-ups, remove it. But if you are missing or losing fish, you should consider adding one.

A plastic trailer behind the spinnerbait is effective as long as it doesn't interfere with the trailer hook. Clunn advises using either a splittail eel or a small ring worm with a curlytail behind the spinnerbait. On big fish waters, however, he opts for a little bigger gator-tail worm trailer.

There are lots of things that can be done with a spinnerbait to improve its fish-catching ability. Tinker and toy with your baits until you come up with something that works. You may be surprised how important "minor" changes can be.

17

Vibrating Baits

C all them sonic plugs, slabs or vibrators; it doesn't matter because bass know them well. Many have had one or more of these lures adorning their lips. The lures all put out a vibrating noise that resembles the sound of injured forage. Bass often react to such a sound with curiosity.

Vibrating baits tend to attract largemouth bass from great distances. Anglers often go to a slab plug when the chips are down and they need to locate bass fast. The lure's action is extremely good in off-color water as well as clear. These plugs catch fish under just about any conditions.

Randy Fite, a bass guide and tournament pro, effectively uses the vibrating baits in waters seven feet deep or shallower. In deeper areas with submerged grass near the surface, though, he uses baits that run very shallow without hard cranking.

Generally, you find small, medium and large vibrating plugs in most manufacturers' lines. Fite prefers the standard or midsize version of vibrating plug in chrome, gold and, in the late spring, baby bass. He considers that color combination extremely effective when winter is on the wane and the bass just start to move up from the depths.

"The fish are extremely dormant," points out Fite. "When they are in the depth range of four to seven feet, the lure is a very effective cold-water bait."

The vibrating plug has an extremely tight wobble that works

effectively at every speed. It retains its action even at very slow speeds. In cold water that's particularly important. Once the water temperature reaches 60 degrees, Fite speeds up his retrieve.

Vegetation Factors

Vibrating baits allow NAFC members to fish vegetation more thoroughly. Spinnerbaits and plastic worms have been the lures of choice when fishing around vegetation. A vibrating bait, however, is also effective along the outer edge of floating plants. Yet when a cast puts the lure in the vegetation, it easily comes out of the weeds.

The speed of retrieve controls the depth achieved by vibrating plugs. Most anglers use a steady retrieve, but a variety of speeds produces maximum results.

A very effective technique for NAFC members is a retrieve that allows the vibrating lure to hang momentarily in the vegetation. When ripped free, the lure draws strikes. If the lure moves too fast over the weeds without hitting any, it is not nearly as effective.

The hooks on most vibrating plugs don't have a good reputation. Because this bait is relatively heavy, anglers often lose a high percentage of their fish on vibrating plugs. Some knowledgeable anglers won't throw one of these baits without first changing the hooks. Some anglers even go to a slightly larger size in the front, which is the most important hook.

To improve the odds of hooking fish, many NAFC members use a soft-action rod and set the drag on the reel very light. Pressuring a fish causes it to jump. With this bait, the fish has about a 50-percent chance of getting off. A soft-tip rod action plus a fairly light drag setting allows the fish to swim down where most bass want to be. That combination makes a big difference in the number of fish actually put in the boat using vibrating plugs.

Vibrating baits are particularly effective over heavy cover when largemouth hold on an outside weedline. Emergent saw grass at the point and scattered, submerged peppergrass off the point can be problems for most lures. Billed crankbaits hit such vegetation after about three cranks and hang up. Even a spinnerbait gets its blade fouled or hung in the grass.

About the only kind of lure to toss under these conditions is a vibrating plug that you can rip out of the peppergrass and continue to retrieve. The vibrating bait can be cast far to reach schoolers that may come up a little farther away.

Feeding Schoolers

A vibrating plug is a good baitfish imitator. It is very effective on schooling bass that are feeding on the major forage, threadfin shad.

Just throw the plug beyond the surface-feeding schools and reel it back fast. This usually triggers aggressive strikes. Vibrating plugs are excellent around grass because they don't dig down and catch in the weeds. You can control the depth by holding the rodtip up or down.

Your lure will achieve more depth if you hold the rod down or keep it high and crank it fast across weedbeds. The lure normally runs true regardless of the speed of retrieve. For deep-water fishing, the vibrating plug is also extremely effective. You have to know how to work it, though.

Vibrating baits tend to lose a high percentage of jumping bass because they are fairly heavy. To combat this problem, the author suggests using a rod with a soft tip and don't pressure the fish into jumping.

Vibrating Baits

Vibrating baits sink fairly quickly and reach the prime mid-depth area where many bass are holding. Let the lure sink to the bottom and then crank it back for maximum action. Some NAFC members fish it deep by pumping it off the bottom.

Activity And Attractions

For best action, use vibrating baits with 10- or 12-pound-test monofilament line. You get a truer action, more depth out of the plugs and more fish strikes.

Larry Nixon often credits his tournament success to vibrating lures. This professional bass angler considers water between 10 and 20 feet deep as the most effective range to pump a vibrating plug along the bottom on structure. His favorite months for employing this tactic are August through October.

"The conditions are right when you locate schooling bass along a creek channel and then a cold front hits, driving them away," explains Nixon. "If you then locate the bass on the bottom, that's when the vibrating plugs will catch them best."

Wise anglers match the size of plug to the size of the baitfish the bass are feeding on. "In the early spring, bass look at tiny shad and bream, so I often throw a ¼-ounce plug," Nixon explains. "I throw the mid-range bait a little later in the year. In the late summer and fall I throw the ¾-ounce bait. If I'm fishing for bigger fish, then I throw the bigger lure."

Nixon's tackle box holds three basic colors of vibrating plugs. He uses a shad imitation such as chrome, a chartreuse with a brown or black back to imitate a bream, and in the spring he uses a fluorescent red to imitate crayfish.

Sliders And Modifications

Nixon likes the new sliding versions of the Rat-L-Trap and Hot Spot. The line goes through the plug and attaches directly to the treble hook hanging below the belly of the plug, which makes it more difficult for bass to throw the plug. For anglers with a gross of older vibrating baits that they don't want to throw away, Nixon suggests a modification that will transform a standard two-treble plug into a slider.

"Take a pair of needle-nosed pliers and extract the line tie

The Rat-L-Trap ProTrap's unique slide-line body allows the lure to slide up the line during a strike, reducing the amount of leverage a fish has to throw a hook.

eye from the lure's back," he explains. "Then pull the front hook and eye out of the plug.

"Now use a small electric drill to make a hole between the two cavities. The bit size should be slightly larger than an ink pen insert. Run the insert through the hole that you drilled into the plug and cut it off flush on each side. Use silicone or epoxy to secure the insert in place."

Nixon then makes a small notch in the bottom of the plug at the insert point, perpendicular to the plug axis. This is done so that the split ring tied directly to the line running through the insert rests up against the bottom of the plug. The vibrating lure will not always track true unless you slice the notch correctly. Finally, the rear hook is removed and a large treble hook is attached to the split ring.

The modification makes the lure run a little shallower, to about three or four feet deep. You won't lose as many fish on these slider lures because this modification allows the plug body to slide free, up and down the line. The fish has only the treble hook to shake free. That's much more difficult without the leverage of a heavy bait.

Vibrating Baits

Buying new sliding, vibrating plugs or making that modification to your existing lures may eliminate some bass losses. I am a strong believer in these plugs and have found them outstanding under many conditions.

Most anyone can catch fish on vibrating plugs. They should be in everyone's tackle box when they're not hanging from a rod!

18

Jigging Variables

T he most overlooked, yet productive, lure of modern times may just be the jig. In the 1950s and early '60s its reign was supreme. Then other types of bait grabbed the imagination of the angling crowd. The jig, however, continued to catch fish.

The bait in its early years was treated as a northern bass lure or one exclusively for cold weather. In the last 10 years it has become known as a year-round bait thanks, in part, to the flippin' technique. Technology has helped jig fishermen into the scientific age of angling. Improvements in jig head design, skirt material and weedguards have been dramatic.

The jig and trailer most resemble a crayfish or, perhaps, a small snake. To that end, most jig and trailer manufacturers offer brown, black and crayfish colors. There are many makers of dark-colored jigs today; Stanley Jigs and Arkie Lures are probably the best known. Executive Tackle, Strike King Lures, Cotee Bait Company, Fishin' Worm Company and a host of others also make bass jigs.

Bait Sizing

Larry Nixon relies heavily on jigs for his success in tournament competition. The Toledo Bend guide and top professional feels that the weight of the jig is an important consideration. The head size Nixon selects depends on water conditions more than anything else.

In its early years the jig was used exclusively in cold water. It took big fish when nothing else would produce.

Fish react the same way in very hot water that they do in very cold water. Extreme temperatures make them sluggish. It takes a slow-falling lure to make a bass strike.

When the water falls below 60 degrees Nixon normally throws a ⅜-ounce (or lighter) bait. The fish's metabolism slows considerably in cold water. Nixon believes the bait should be slowed down accordingly. The lighter baits accomplish that job and net more strikes.

Between 60 and 75 degrees bass still hit a smaller bait, but the pro often goes to a heavier jig. Nixon says that he covers a little more water with a ½-ounce jig and that his casts are more accurate.

If the wind is blowing you'll have to use a heavier bait. That helps keep the jig on the bottom within the strike zone for a longer period.

At some point between 70 and 80 degrees the fish will sometimes stop hitting jigs, according to Nixon. They've seen a lot of jigs thrown at them throughout the spring. The angler should then go to a very heavy jig, ½ ounce or larger, to get it down fast. That should trigger strikes.

Hook Happenings

There are a variety of hook shapes and sizes donning lead heads today. Stanley makes jigs with flippin' hooks or casting hooks. Anglers use the former primarily when flippin' brush or shallow-water structure in waters less than 10 feet deep.

When an angler is using 10- to 17-pound-test line and a medium-heavy-action rod, he should stay with the casting-size hook. Stanley's 3/0 casting hook is a smaller diameter hook than its flippin' hook. It penetrates well.

"So many times you don't feel strikes on a jig," says Nixon. "You more or less pick up on it and there's something 'there.' Then you realize that it's a fish and you don't get a real good hookset. With the smaller diameter casting hook, you don't need a great hookset to get a solid hookup."

Trailer Thoughts

Nixon uses a pig trailer about 80 percent of the time. Anytime the water temperature is less than 68 degrees, Nixon will use the pork.

"Bass take jigs as they fall," explains Nixon. "With pork,

Now anglers are turning to the jig during the hot summer months. Flippin' jigs under docks or along shoreline structure is especially effective.

they get a better bite and hold onto the bait longer."

There are three porks from Uncle Josh that work well on jigs, according to Nixon. The No. 11 frog is a smaller, more compact bait suitable for fishing in waters that may have bass in the 1- to 2-pound range. Use the No. 1 frog when flippin' for large bass with a long rod and heavy jig. The 800 Spring Lizard is also a good choice when looking for big bass. It provides a little bit more bulk without being too long.

When using pork as a trailer, experienced anglers often take a ¼-inch-long piece of plastic worm and slip it up on the hook to keep the pork from rolling back.

In the hands of an experienced angler with confidence in it, the jig and pig is a deadly bait. Nixon likes to use it about 80 percent of the time for cooler water conditions and larger fish. The other 20 percent of the time he chooses the Stanley 4-inch Crawworm that comes packaged with the jigs for the trailer addition.

"If I could use plastic all the time and get away with it, I probably would," he says. "I usually stick with a black or brown Crawworm with a little tint to the claws, such as fire or blue."

Colorful Combinations

The trailer chosen is generally the same color as the jig, and the same criteria apply. Off-colored water dictates a black or dark trailer. If the water is clear, see-through colors are preferred. As is often the case with lures, trailer color choice may be based on a confidence factor beyond the water color.

Nixon's color choice for the jig is normally determined by the water color. In darker colored water, he uses either a black jig or one with a fluorescent tip, such as a fire or chartreuse tail. The added color makes the bait more visible to the fish.

"I like the contrast of the two-tone jig skirts," says Nixon. "They are the greatest things that ever happened to jig fishing. You now have the metal flake colors that work so well on the worm available on the jig."

Crayfish are normally darker in color in the darker water, and that's one reason many anglers prefer a dark-colored jig. In dark or off-color waters you can only see down about 18 inches from the surface. In waters with clarity of four or five feet, a brown jig or one of the new flake colors works well.

Jigs are excellent big-bass baits. Pros often turn to them when bigger fish are needed to win a tournament.

Jigging Variables

Summer Locals

Heavy cover is the best area in which to use jigs during hot weather. It's a time when you have to put the bait right in front of the fish. It takes the right cast into a brush pile or grassbed to attract a strike.

Boat docks, pilings, logs and the like are prime summertime targets. In hot weather, casts should be extremely short. The real key to summer jig angling success is a good presentation. You have to put the jig right on top of the fish because they are not really feeding. They are more or less guarding their territory.

Many bass professionals consider the jig a dependable bait they can call upon all year long to catch fish. I've found the same to be true. In my estimation it deserves much more credit than it usually gets. It's a winner!

19

Native Shiners

Golden shiners are by far the most popular live bait for largemouth bass fishing and for a good reason. Bass love them—they also hate them. Lunker bass like to eat substantial forage most of the year and shiners fit the bill. During bedding time, however, the bass frequently compete with the ever-present shiner. Spawning movements stir bottom sediment. Shiners pick up the scent and move in to feast. Both male and female bass attempt to chase off the persistent and hungry minnows and use whatever force is necessary to do so.

For this reason the shiner is a good choice for springtime trophy bass action. While they are an excellent year-round bait, shiners are an especially good choice during the cooler months because their metabolism closely tracks that of the bass. Cold-water bass are sluggish and so are shiners during this time of the year.

The family of shiners is distributed throughout the states in lakes, sluggish rivers and in small ponds. Most bodies of water have one or more varieties. Some of the more numerous kinds of shiners include the golden, common, spottail and emerald.

In the spring, the deep-bodied golden shiner exhibits a gold-color tint that is easily recognizable. They are the hardiest of the clan and grow up to 14 or 16 inches, making them a great trophy bass bait. Their range includes most of the eastern two-thirds of the United States, and you can find them in waters from small ponds to large impoundments.

The common shiners are broad-bodied and high-backed. They prefer moving water and you generally find them in the same states as the golden. The spottail shiner and emerald shiner are the "weak sisters" of the common and golden shiners. They are least hardy of the family due to their oxygen and temperature requirements. The slender emerald shiner and the spottail, named for the black spot at the base of the tail, are among the prettiest of all minnows and easy targets for marauding bass.

Spawn Interaction

In late winter and spring, shiners frequent bass spawning grounds. Although they are primarily food fish, shiners are mortal enemies of the female largemouth during the spawn. I first used shiners for bait many springs ago in Florida. It was an interesting experience.

The bobber danced around on the surface and disappeared occasionally during the shiner's first minutes in the water. Then it slowed to a methodical swim over the area. My partner placed his shiner out in another direction to better cover the area. The shiners both worked well, as evidenced by the bobbers traveling in and out and back and forth.

Although we saw no evidence of any action from surrounding boats, my bobber disappeared within a few minutes. I fed line out fast at first. Then, as the bass slowed to swallow her catch, I reeled fast until the line became taut and set the hook. I kept heavy pressure on her as she headed through the sparse weeds parallel to the boat.

Steady pressure finally turned her, and I brought her out of the vegetation and toward the boat. The huge bass rolled into the net, and I leaned back into my chair momentarily exhausted. My partner held up the beautiful 9½-pound bass for me to admire.

Exuberant over my first bass of the day, I chose another likely looking shiner from the livebox and tossed it in the same general area. Within minutes the bobber again disappeared. The rod bowed and my heavy baitcasting tackle soon tired the twin of my first catch. Soon, the pair were finning easily on the gunwale-mounted stringer.

Golden shiners are the most popular live bait for largemouth fishing for good reason—big bass love 'em!

Native Shiners

The water conditions that March day were nearly perfect for the day's catch, which included two other largemouth more than 6 pounds. Several other trophy bass that have succumbed to the big shiner baits over the years have also left me with fond memories.

Shiner Connection

Shiners inhabit densely weeded and protected waters during most of the year. They love small canals and sloughs just off larger bodies of water. To check for this kind of forage, toss out a few bread crumbs. If any shiners are around, they'll soon feed on the bread.

Usually the best area to fish for bass is right where the bait is thickest. Shiners are there to feed on their forage—plankton. Many anglers take a small hook and cane pole and catch their own bait.

In fact, most well-equipped fishing guides who regularly use large river shiners in Florida's big bass waters catch their own. They normally supply their parties with five or six dozen lively baitfish from the boat's bubbly livebox. At $5 to $7 for a dozen of the finest, an average day's investment may cost more than some anglers can afford.

Two anglers easily use 40 to 50 shiners a day, but they may need nine or 10 dozen shiners if the weather is hot. Shiners are not particularly hardy, especially in high temperatures. Anglers must either pay the price and stock up with bait (if available) or catch their own. It's much cheaper to do the latter and even kind of fun.

There are two ways to catch your own shiners. The most productive is via cast net. It requires the most in equipment cost at about $100 to $150 for a good quality six- to seven-foot radius net. Instead, you can invest $10 or $15 for a cane pole with small hook and bobber, and catch them one at a time.

Where To Look

Shiners can normally be found on the edge of moss or eelgrass, close to moving water. They eat algae, so look for large schools where algae abounds. An algae film can be found on eelgrass in some of the better areas.

Shiners can be particularly hard to catch or lure near the

range of a cast net in very clear water, and fishing for them is definitely slower on a full moon than during other lunar phases. Early and late in the day are the most productive times to catch large shiners, but they can be easily caught over chummed and baited holes all day long.

The size of the first shiners caught generally reveals the typical size of most in the school. All specimens from highly oxygenated water require continuous aeration once on board.

Bait And Chum

The first step in the shiner-catching process for NAFC members is attracting them to an area by baiting it. Do this with one of a variety of good baits such as soybean cake, hog or rabbit pellets, dog food or anything with cereal in it. Even canned dog food with a couple of holes punched in the can to allow seepage attracts shiners to an area.

Toss the cereal bait into an area relatively free of weeds in about six feet of water for a cast net operation, and 10 to 12 feet of water for the cane pole fishing method. Find the best areas by simply baiting about a dozen areas and trying them all the next day to find the four to six that normally produce. Then, rebait the two or three best holes for good results the following day.

You often see shiners feeding on the surface in the pockets of heavy weedbeds near the baited area, but bait-seeking NAFC members cannot normally get there without scaring the baitfish away. It is fairly easy, however, to bring them up to the boat by chumming.

While effective baiting requires 24 hours to attract a school of shiners to an area, chumming produces in a few minutes. Quick oats, regular oatmeal or bread crumbs mixed with water and dumped upcurrent from the baited hole brings the shiners swimming.

Catching Them

The cane pole is the most common method of catching shiners and a bread ball the size of a BB is the preferred bait. The bread should be moist in order to form a good ball and the hook size can vary from No. 12 to 16. Guides normally use a long-shank No. 14 hook for ease of extraction from a hooked baitfish. This hook is less apt to injure and kill the shiner. A fish bleeding from the gills normally dies quickly and should be discarded.

The bait should fall to about four feet below the small bobber. When the bobber disappears, lift the cane pole, swing the shiner aboard the boat and quickly deposit it in an aerated livewell. When the shiners are hitting well, use a small, white plastic worm instead of bread for good results.

Anglers with access to a cast net round up several dozen shiners more quickly than they do with a cane pole. Four dozen of the baitfish normally can be netted in an hour or so over a baited area. The net works best over holes totally devoid of vegetation because heavy weeds interfere with the net's closing. It can be cast deeper (up to 10 feet) in dark, stained waters or on very cloudy days. Conversely, clear waters and high, noon-bright sunlight require a quicker net opening and shallower areas to load the boat with bait.

Shiner Care

Shiner baits are very valuable and deserve great care. To keep shiners fresh and lively, professionals normally use aerators

Shiners are expensive to buy. NAFC members can keep costs down by catching their own bait.

and a special granular chemical developed by big-bass specialists Doug Hannon and Tony Wheeler of Sanford, Florida's, Jungle Labs.

When avid bass fisherman Tony Wheeler assumed management duties of the Jungle Laboratories Corporation in 1980, he had an idea for marketing a product aimed at anglers hoping to keep dozens of shiners alive in the small livewells common in most boats. Working with Hannon, Wheeler and his staff, he developed Shiner Life and Bait Life. They also market Catch and Release, which is more highly concentrated than the other two.

The ingredients contain a tranquilizer, a stimulator of protective slime production and a bacteria killer. The chemical actually increases the oxygen in the water and prevents fungus growth. Bass can even be dunked in the baitwell for a few minutes prior to their release. The treatment speeds up their recovery from possible parasite infection, handling stress and other problems.

Taking Enough Bait

Taking care of the bait is an important ingredient in a successful bass trip. So is having enough. I was on a central Florida lake in January a few years back and ran out of big shiners. But that did not stop my partner and I from catching some nice fish.

It had been very cold during the month so the bass hadn't even thought about their spawning activities. They still held in relatively deep water on a hyacinth line. My partner and I were fishing for Florida bass of the hawg variety. I chose the large shiners as our best bet to seduce a cold-water lunker in a limited amount of time.

Once on the lake, we moved quickly to a hyacinth jam and rigged our baits with 5/0 hooks through the lips of 10-inch shiners. Small split shot kept them down and away from the hyacinth roots and large cigar-shaped bobbers. We waited only five minutes when my cork 'popped' under.

I let the fish run for about eight or 10 seconds and set the hook. The stiff rod strained and the reel's drag moaned momentarily until I headed the monster my way. My 20-pound-test line held and my partner adeptly handled the net, lifting the huge bass into the boat.

She weighed 12 pounds, 2 ounces that afternoon when she hit the scales. That started a great day for me. Although my partner couldn't seem to hook a fish, I placed seven bass in the livewell that totaled 32 pounds. To this day it's still one of my better efforts on the water.

That bass was my largest to date, and I owe it to a big native shiner. I took all seven of the fish from the hyacinth line in seven to eight feet of water and caught all on the shiners. I took the small 3-pounders on the smaller 5-inch shiners that we were forced to use after our supply of large shiners ran out!

The shiner is without a doubt the best big-bass bait in the southern United States. More bass lures have been painted to imitate shiners than any other forage. Before the naturalized lures were introduced, the shiner color was on more plugs than even the shad, which has itself come on tremendously strong in the past few years.

=20=

The Manageable Shad

Elroy Krueger looked up from his chart recorder. A professional bass angler from San Antonio, Texas, Krueger and I were chasing bass on a power plant lake near that city. The late-fall weather had been chilly for a straight week with air temperatures plummeting to the low thirties each night.

"We'll have to wait for the shad to move to the surface before the bass will turn on," he explained. "Right now, they're on the bottom in the channel and I can't even mark a bigger fish."

The cold weather had driven the shad deeper into the warm discharge water that ran through an old creek channel some 40 feet beneath the surface of the cooling reservoir. Vast schools of threadfin covered the 10-foot-deep channel from one bank to the other, as indicated by the recorder. Thousands of the fish blackened the chart just above the bottom contour line.

In weather like this, shad normally move off the bottom toward the surface by midmorning as the sun warms the upper layers of water. Winterkills of shad are usually negligible in power plant reservoirs with heated discharge water. Shad depend on this warm water source during the cooler months.

That morning was colder than most and a heavy fog insulated the surface water from the warm sun rays until late in the morning. Around 1 p.m., the shad schools moved toward the surface as Krueger predicted. First a few came up, and then several headed toward the warming surface water.

Streaks showing the upward movement of the baitfish burned into the chart paper. Soon, larger individual fish showed up on the chart recorder at a position about 15 feet below the newly formed shad schools near the lake's surface.

Gradually, the recorder found the majority of the shad near the surface and several bass began feeding at around 15- to 20-foot depths on strays making their way up to the school. Large schools of feeding bass never really formed before I had to leave, but we managed to take several nice largemouth, the biggest around 3½ pounds. After pictures, we released them to once again chase the roaming schools of shad.

Threadfin shad are a favorite morsel of the largemouth bass. They grow to only a few inches and are more manageable than their cousin, the gizzard shad. Gizzard shad outgrow most of their predator fish in a year or two. Threadfin remain a more edible size for the duration of their lives.

Threadfin shad thrive in huge schools, which abound in most of the country's southern reservoirs and lakes. They are susceptible to the cold but can survive in deep-water lakes and heated power plant waters.

Their cold-temperature sensitivity is important to anglers because it helps them locate the schools of shad with the aid of either a water temperature gauge or a sonar unit. It is essential to know how to use those tools to find shad. A depthfinder or chart recorder can be the key to success when searching for the favorite bass forage fish.

Reservoir Nomads
Shad rove the channels feeding on plankton and insect larvae. They usually concentrate within five feet of the lake's surface while feeding because sunlight promotes the growth of plankton. The water temperature, however, has to be tolerable for them to be at the surface.

At times, huge schools of shad appear right on the surface, moving about in their feeding. On a calm lake their presence can hardly go undetected. They usually avoid heavy cover because bass may be waiting in ambush and instead move randomly about.

The little, 2- to 3-inch threadfins make small ripples on the

A good sonar unit is vital for locating the roaming schools of shad—and bass—in open water.

The Manageable Shad

surface as they cavort. When spooked, the school seems to explode on the surface and disappears into the depths, usually returning only a few yards away. Seagulls notice this action. They also love to feed on these fish. The gulls and other water birds swoop at the shad from above, which may just drive them down to the depths of the bass.

You usually find largemouth bass 12 to 25 feet down, beneath the shad schools. When they get the urge to feed, they simply move up. The bass drive the shad into an excited frenzy as they try to escape the slashing bass. Dramatic surface disturbances often occur as the bass boil and swirl in the baitfish schools, knocking several shad into the air.

The bass often feed until they're full, then cough up some and go for more. They leave maimed and crippled shad on the surface in the wake of the disaster as the remainder of the school flees in panic. The wounded members of the shad tribe that escape the bass feeding mayhem probably end up on a fatal flight with a waiting sea gull.

Bird Spotting

The gull, like the bass, is never far away from the schools of shad. Gulls easily spot schools of shad from the air on a sunny day, and knowing where the gulls are helps an angler pinpoint the forage and the bass.

In the cooler months, from fall through the first part of spring, finding the area of the lake where the gulls are working or just resting is important. The resting gulls usually sit over schools of shad, waiting for bass to start feeding from below, thereby driving them up.

Bass herd these schools of shad around the lake, periodically slashing at them and turning the surface water into foam. They attack the shad near submerged creek or river channel bends, near the edges of flooded timber stands, in boat lanes, through heavy cover and on underwater islands or humps on the lake bottom. They wait in nearby cover for these schools to wander by and then pop them.

Shad use the submerged creek channels and boat lanes to travel around the lake. They try to stay away from their predators at the edge of the timber, but it is not always easy. They travel the underwater paths, which may lead them through bridges, where they are again more out in the open and easy targets for largemouth.

In such tight quarters, the shad are very spooky. And justly so. Once bass have attacked one school, they simply retreat to their hideaway and wait for the next shad school to swim past. In more open water the bass may simply fall back to a suspended position just below the feeding zone and wait for another school of shad to meander within range.

All this surface action occurs year-round. The bass schooling activity happens in June and July on Lake Livingston and yet, the lakes near San Antonio, just a hundred miles or so away, are better in September and October.

I've seen bass schooling in August on Table Rock Lake in Missouri, in November on Santee Cooper in South Carolina and in April on Blue Cypress Lake in central Florida. I've also caught bass feeding on surface schools of shad in January on one of the world's better bass lakes, Lake Guerrero in Mexico.

The threadfin shad ranges from Guatemala and Belize in Central America, north to Ohio and Pennsylvania. You find them from Florida west, along the Gulf Coast drainage to California. Oklahoma, Tennessee, Arizona and even Hawaii have populations of threadfin. They're not strictly a southern forage fish.

Thermal Limitation

The shad's range-limiting factor is their vulnerability to cold water. Biologists have found that shad mortality starts at about 44 degrees in the southern states. Acclimated shad populations in lakes farther north may tolerate a slightly lower temperature.

Bass don't feel much like feeding at these temperatures, but when things warm up a bit, the threadfin forage will be needed badly. Oklahoma fish and game biologists have found that bass in the Canton Reservoir prefer a diet of only shad in the winter. Stomach analysis reveals that bass consume three or four percent of their body weight in shad each day.

The shad's susceptibility to cold water concentrates them in warm waters during winter months. This provides largemouth with easy pickin's, according to Texas Parks and Wildlife Department biologist Alan Wenger.

"The shad population tends to move into the heated

discharge waters of many of our power plant reservoirs," says Wenger. "And that makes feeding easier for the bass."

Although limited by water temperature, the threadfin tolerate various salt contents. You find them in almost pure freshwater lakes like Lake Livingston in Texas. They also do well in brackish tributaries along the Gulf Coast, according to Wenger. They can survive in waters of 10 to 20 parts per thousand salt content. The Gulf of Mexico is around 30 parts per thousand.

The threadfin has a short life span, which limits its growth. A two-year life span is normal for the fish and a maximum length of 5 inches is about tops for the northern-based threadfin. In the southern states they may reach 7 inches, but these giants are very rare. The 2- or 3-incher is most common in the lakes I've been on regardless of how much plankton is available for food.

Wind And Current Influences

Shad follow and feed on drifting plankton. As the next step in the food chain, bass won't be far behind. Plankton drifts toward shore with a steady wind, so you can occasionally find threadfin in shallow waters.

The wind and wave action also filters the sun's rays and allows the shad to feed nearer the surface than normal. Since the water clarity and light rays determine how deep the shad will be, wave action is just what the bass angler needs.

The wave action piles up schools of shad on shallow points. Bass simply move up from the deep after them. Shad schools are so large that high winds push them near (and sometimes onto) the shoreline. The lower light penetration brings them closer to the surface to feed and gamefish follow suit.

Plankton and minute organic matter drift not only with the wind, but also with the current. Due to its light weight, you normally find this matter near the surface. Shad move in such currents to feed and bass follow the forage.

Current sweeps through bridges, along submerged creek channels and even in unexpected places on a lake. The current in heated discharge waters from power plants provides an additional attraction for the threadfin—food!

Shad normally face into the current while feeding on

plankton. An angler can determine a slight current by noting the direction of the schools of shad travel. The current in some reservoirs fluctuates according to whether or not the turbines at the dam are running. Lake drawdowns and even navigational lock use affect a current in some lakes. This often triggers bass into a feeding spree on the hapless shad.

Fishing The Schools

NAFC members hoping to follow the forage and connect on some nice bass should take several precautions once they locate their quarry. First of all, both the threadfin and the bass hate noise. Excessive boat or motor noise drives both species deeper. Spooking one fish generally eliminates the school from the angler's view. If bass are working the shad on top, the action could stop completely.

An angler in the schooling action should land each bass quickly and keep noise to a bare minimum. Any disturbance of the school shuts off its activity and the angler's.

Schooling activity can sometimes be great for the angler. In other cases, the shad and bass sound a warning before the angler reaches them. The latter is probably the rule rather than the

Locating and fishing near schools of shad will reap big rewards.

The Manageable Shad

exception for upper St. John's River bass in north Florida, near Palatka. There is often schooling activity there, but seldom do the fishermen connect.

The bass chase shad all over the river, but unless your lure hits near a breaking fish, forget about fried fillets. It takes too long to switch lures for schooling activity. An angler needs to have handy a school-bass rod rigged with a heavy shad-like lure. A tail spinner lure, such as a "Little George," is ideal for those 200-foot casts that may be required to hit a breaking fish.

Bass usually corral the shad in the river near bends and at creek inlets. I find that the most successful way to cash in on the action is to sit in the middle of the inlet and fish the drops, down into deep water. A shad imitation fished along the river bottom in deep water lures some of the up-and-down bass to the stringer. Drops always exist where there is surface activity because the bass cannot attack the shad schools so easily in open water.

An angler should match the lure size to the size of shad the bass are eating. Work the lure slowly beneath the area where the surface activity occurs. If you can't catch the eager school bass while they slaughter the defenseless shad on top, keep your patience and try them deep.

Surface action occurs more prominently in the summer months in many lakes. Some waters produce this activity during months with negligible winds and warm surface water. An angler should always be alert for gull activity, which indicates that schools of shad are below, and so are the bass. Following on the trail of sea gulls and shad schools roving about the lake leads to exciting and rewarding fishing.

21

The Underrated Crayfish

When Californian Ray Easley caught the second largest bass ever, a 21-pound, 3-ounce largemouth, from Ventura County's Lake Casitas in 1980, the bassing world took notice. Easley caught the prize on a live crayfish. The small, lobster-like crustacean has regained prominence as a premier bait for big bass. After Easley's catch, trophy bass seekers everywhere began requesting the crayfish at bait shops. Lure makers hurried to develop or refine artificial crayfish crankbaits.

Whether you call them crawdads, crawfish or crayfish, they're one and the same to a largemouth, smallmouth or spotted bass. These fish love them. The plentiful crayfish provide bass with a food source higher in protein and other nutrients than forage fish. A bass generally does not have to spend a lot of energy catching a small crayfish scurrying backwards among the rocks and weeds. The crayfish's short bursts of speed, poor eyesight and lack of stamina make this ugly creature relatively easy for the bass to capture.

Another reason crayfish are so popular with bass is their perennial availability in lakes, ponds and rivers in many parts of the country. Various sources list the number of crayfish species and subspecies in North America between 100 and 200. The numerous little crustaceans often comprise the major food source for smallmouth, spotted bass and Suwannee bass. Even largemouth bass in certain environments and at specific times of the year dine almost exclusively on crayfish.

The larger a bass grows, the more likely it is to devour crayfish. Samplings of adult bass stomach contents at various times of the year reveal that in many waters, crayfish constitute some two-thirds of the diet. If you pay close attention to the stomach contents of the bass you clean, you'll more than likely find two, three or possibly more skeletal remains of the tempting crayfish.

Stomach Survey

During the first week of March a few years ago, I was on a small southern lake that had an apparent overabundance of crayfish. A week before a small fishing club contest, my fishing partner and I had taken some nice bass in pretournament practice. Another club member hadn't fared as well but did manage to catch a few nice-sized largemouth for his supper.

My partner and I cleaned four bass each and examined their stomach contents during the operation. We found their bellies stuffed with small, 1-inch-long crayfish, six or eight per fish. During the week prior to the Saturday tournament we searched tackle boxes and stores, trying to come up with a good replica of the crusty forage. At the time lure manufacturers had not jumped into the craze for natural imitations and an exact replica was unavailable.

We were able to round up a few similar lures. Although they were about twice as long as real crayfish, we managed to take third and fourth places in the contest. However, the other angler who had previewed the lake one week earlier had also surveyed the stomach contents of the bass he had taken. He and his tournament partner spent all week building a mold and pouring dozens of almost perfect replicas of the crayfish. The coloring, size and shape of their creations allowed them to win the top two spots in that tournament.

Food Search

Crayfish grow much larger than the average 1-inch-long populace we encountered in that lake at that time. After they reach 5 inches their forage value to bass decreases substantially. They grow to that size over a four- or five-year life span. Crayfish are primarily nocturnal creatures and prefer low light

Baits that imitate crayfish are excellent bass catchers. NAFC members have a wide variety of artificials to choose from.

The Underrated Crayfish

levels in which to move about and feed. They do feed occasionally during daylight hours but for the most part are very cautious in their movements, staying between rocks, under leaves, in ledge crevices and through weedbeds.

Crayfish generally hide under logs, rocks, weeds or other protective cover. Their diet, found around the bottom habitat, consists of both vegetable and animal matter. They are scavengers that live on whatever they can grab. Eelgrass, algae, plankton and tiny snails make up a part of their intake, as do small minnows and decomposing animal life. They are also cannibalistic, preying on smaller members of their own species. They are not sufficiently agile to capture a great deal of other food alive.

When searching for food, crayfish may crawl in any direction but mainly go forward. The large claws are normally used to tear food into edible portions.

Crayfish also use their claws to burrow into the mud to survive periods of drought or cold. When temperatures rise into the high 50s, however, the crustaceans pop out into the predator-prey cycle once again.

Confrontations

Without the pincers, crayfish are unable to fend off attackers. Bass that spot a crayfish moving over bottom debris will stalk the prey. The confrontation will usually result in the crayfish snapping its claws menacingly at the predator. The standoff is normally temporary, and when the cautious bass musters the inclination to strike, it will do so quickly.

If the crayfish stands its ground rather than fleeing, it will more than likely lose a pincer. Normally, the bass quickly tries to disarm the prey by removing a raised claw. It will seize the crayfish by the pincer and shake it violently until the claw breaks off. The bass will often eject the claw and try to remove the second one the same way. Once declawed, the prey is eaten quickly.

This ritual is generally followed by bass in the 1- to 3-pound range. Small bass will occasionally gobble up a crayfish, claws and all. The small, 2-inch variety and soft-shelled crayfish are most susceptible to being engulfed fully armed by a bass. Lunker bass will literally suck in a hapless crayfish from a foot away.

Crayfish love rock areas in lakes and streams—so do bass, particularly smallmouth and spotted bass. Crayfish imitations work great in these areas.

The Underrated Crayfish

Large bass waste little time or energy messing with the removal of armament. My experience in stomach-sampling over the years tends to bear this out. Skeletal remains in larger bass usually include at least one pincer. Small bass stomach contents usually have no such appendage when stuffed with a 3-inch or longer crayfish.

Growth Molting

Not only are the claws and legs regenerative but so is the crayfish's armor-like outer shell. As it grows, the shell must be shed and regrown continually. This shedding of the skeleton, or molting, occurs more often in the young as they grow into adults. The crayfish simply outgrows its shell, splits it open and crawls out. This happens from two to 12 times each year, depending on water temperature, chemistry and age.

The entire molting process may take a couple of days. As the hard encasement weakens in preparation for peeling and the growth of a new external skeleton, the crayfish emits a hormone scent that attracts predators. The crayfish has an extreme requirement for calcium at this time. It actually absorbs calcium into the body organs from the hard shell being discarded. This weakens the old coat but the crayfish needs that calcium for formation of a larger garment. Cannibalism occurs more frequently during the molting stage as the crayfish attempts to satisfy its requirement for additional calcium.

The hard shell of the crayfish prior to peeling will usually turn dark brown or black and the decaying coat often exhibits a rough finish from parasite attachments. Once the old shell is shed the soft-shelled crayfish is helpless and vulnerable to all predators. The texture of the new shell is soft and jelly-like. Its external coloration is pale and transparent.

Soft-shelled crayfish are definitely a delicacy for bass. For live-bait fishermen, they are the choice by a landslide. This excellent bait is often difficult to find, but with it comes a big-bass guarantee. The first time I discovered a "softy" in my 12-foot seine about 25 years ago I thought it was a decomposing crustacean. Fortunately, I didn't toss it back. It caught a 2-pound bass for me!

Crayfish can be gently squeezed to determine whether or not they are molting. If the shell cracks easily, the crayfish can be peeled and used for bait immediately. Or it can be put in a bait box and allowed to shed the coat naturally, which occurs within a few days.

As the soft shell begins absorbing calcium from the internal organs (primarily through the blood), the new skeleton hardens. The shell toughens as the crayfish gains strength to again mobilize and defend itself against some predators. At this stage the crayfish is an exceptional bait, able to fight off small predators yet truly a morsel for the bass.

The molting process is concluded when the overcoat hardens to a slick, tough texture. The crayfish is fully capable of defense and offense with its armament. At this stage the crayfish makes the poorest bait. Crayfish in various stages of molting are best for bait. But crayfish are more abundant in hard shells, and these should be used rather than discarded.

My father introduced me to fishing live crayfish for bass in the late 1950s on an Ozark lake. He bought a couple dozen "crawdads" and anchored on a brushy, rock-strewn point one evening. The tail-hooked bait occasionally found its way into rock crevices. But our stringer, after fishing the last two hours of daylight, was impressive. A half-dozen smallmouth bass and one largemouth pushing 3 pounds made our trip to that lake memorable.

Ultimate Crayfish Lovers

Crayfish like rocky areas in lakes and streams and so do bass, particularly smallmouth and spotted bass. These two major species of bass may be the ultimate crayfish lovers. Their distribution is in most major river systems and in many hill country reservoirs throughout the states. They prefer stream-like areas such as steep, sloping banks and points with rock and gravel substrata where forage is abundant. Riprap along dams and road embankments often attracts smallmouth and spotted bass because small currents wash hapless crayfish their way.

There are actually several species of spotted bass in the United States with the Kentucky being the most widespread. The smaller Guadalupe spotted bass, a species unique to Texas and found only in the Guadalupe, Colorado and San Antonio rivers and their tributaries, loves the crustaceans also.

Habitat preference is a key in knowing where to look for

Today's crayfish imitations are so lifelike they are nearly impossible to distinguish from the real thing.

spotted bass. The stream heritage is evident in their feeding habits. They prefer insects, mollusks and crustaceans. One of the most irresistible baits is the crayfish.

Live crayfish baits are often good in stream-type areas due to the alkaline level of the water. Rocky areas high in lime content have a higher pH value (more alkaline), which is often conducive to frequent molting. This means that soft-shelled crayfish are more numerous, and there is a good chance that the bass will feed heavily on such forage.

Check the area adjacent to the water for hardwood trees such as cypress, oak, aspen and magnolia instead of pine. The former denote a higher pH. Exceptionally clear water year-round is indicative of acidic water (low pH). Crayfish prefer a pH of 7.3 to 7.8, while largemouth and smallmouth bass prefer a range of 7.5 to 7.9 and 7.9 to 8.2, respectively.

Limestone Bass Food

Limestone outcroppings such as those found in northern Florida and southern Georgia are evidence of water with high alkaline content. An example is the Suwannee River water-shed. It has numerous swift, rocky stretches that are full of crayfish. The river and its tributaries also contain the crustacean-loving Suwannee bass, a rare species endemic to that watershed.

These short, chunky fish closely resemble smallmouth bass. They seldom exceed 12 inches. The Suwannee bass has a bluish lower jaw and brown sides with diamond-shaped blotches. It hangs out in shoal areas where exposed irregular limestone or limestone rubble is prominent. It feeds in areas where eddies meet fast waters or where underwater drop-offs buffer the current.

Stomach analyses have shown that crayfish comprise about 80 percent of Suwannees' diet. Knowing this dining character-istic, I was recently able to establish a line-class world record for the little bass with a crayfish-painted crankbait, the Mann Crawdad. A friend accompanying me also established a line-class record with the World Freshwater Fishing Hall of Fame in Hayward, Wisconsin. Our plugs were cast to the crayfish-laden shoals and worked back along the rocky bottom to entice the action.

The calcareous springwater introduced through the lime-stone substrate is extremely attractive to crayfish. The geological and chemical features of water quality, environmental stability and narrow water temperature range make these waters prime for crayfish lovers and for anglers in search of them. Float trips down such waters in the South on a summer day can result in beautiful catches of both smallmouth and largemouth bass. On the Suwannee River you'll catch three or four times as many largemouth bass as you will other bass species. You will do as well on other rivers too, where spotted bass, redeye and smallmouth are numerous.

Baiting Up

Crayfish can be used as effective bass bait through several hooking arrangements. Glue is often used to affix the crustacean to a 3/0 or 4/0 hook. Place a drop of quick-drying glue and the hook on the crayfish shell, add another drop of glue and wait a minute or so if you have live bait with full mobility. Two small rubber bands can also be used to secure the bait. One band goes around its midsection. The other is fitted over the pincers and head to tightly hold the hook, which is threaded under the bands. The point of the hook is positioned to lie against the crayfish's side. The rotating hook will ensure a hookup when it comes in contact with a bass.

The crayfish can also be impaled on the hook. A popular method is to run the short-shank, 4/0 weedless hook through the last joint of the tail with the hook point up. Hooking it through the center or upper part of the body can damage internal organs causing quick death. When hooked mid-tail, the natural movement of the crayfish is inhibited. Since crayfish travel quickly the hooking should allow movement. The bait can crawl forward on the bottom and be pulled free of any temporary hangups it finds.

Fish the crayfish on the bottom with as small a weight as possible. A single split shot about a foot from the bait should suffice without limiting the crayfish's movement. A small slip sinker rigged behind a swivel and 12-inch leader is also a popular rig for areas with current.

Often a crayfish will crawl under logs or rocks for concealment and hang onto the obstruction with its pincers. I prefer to disarm it by crushing the pincers and leaving them on the bait. The claws become ineffective in warding off bass or hanging onto tangles. It will still wave the pincers, but a bass won't be held off from its meal as long. This is particularly important on hard-shell crayfish.

Hardshells with full armament are especially adept at getting hung up when fished on bottom terrain. To make them more productive, try stripping off several segments of the outer tail skin at the front, leaving the rear two sections for maintaining hook implantation.

When still fishing a sloping bank with cover, tug on the crayfish every 20 to 30 seconds to keep it out of mischief. A slow, constant retrieve will also work. Remember, the slower the better with this live bait. When a bass inhales the crayfish, go ahead and set the hook. Most baits are bite-sized and will fit inside a bass' mouth.

Catching And Storing Crayfish

For those NAFC members who want to catch their own, the crayfish is relatively easy to capture. There are a variety of methods that work and probably the easiest is to seine them. Roadside ditches, small sloughs and muddy ponds are excellent places to pull a 14-foot seine. The net should be kept firmly on the bottom as two people slowly move it through heavy weedbeds, rocks and mud in water less than three feet deep.

Often two or three dozen crayfish are captured with a single pull of only 20 feet or so. In streams, place the seine across the current and, if legal in your state, stir up the rocks and vegetation downstream with a garden rake, a hoe or your feet. The crayfish flushed from hiding will scurry upstream and end up in the net. If moving the seine in flowing water, work downstream with the net for maximum take. The rake can also be used to drag weeds onto the bank to check for concealed crayfish.

Rocks in clear water can be turned over by hand in search of crayfish burrows. Confused inhabitants can be grabbed or dip-netted. At night a spotlight in the shallows can reveal big crayfish active all over the bottom. They can be caught easily by fishing for them after dark or in muddy water during daylight hours. Hook a piece of liver, bacon, lunch meat, fish meat or any meat scrap onto a string and lower it into a culvert or other dark, muddy water hole. Pull the bait out slowly and you should have a few hanging onto it. Grab them quickly after slipping them onto shore.

The final way to catch a bunch of the critters is to use baited crayfish traps, wire boxes with a conical hole in one end and bait inside. Leave it in a shallow pond or rock-strewn flat overnight with bait of fish scraps or rotten vegetables as the attraction. Check regulations for restrictions on the trap and for laws concerning removing live bait from local waters.

Once you have a mess of crayfish, storing them is easy. A Styrofoam cooler with an inch of water in the bottom and plenty of peat moss or weeds will keep them happy. Use ice to keep them cool. Or refrigerate them overnight for the best-conditioned bait. If pincers are large and space is small, disarm them because they'll want to fight each other. Keep the soft-shelled crayfish separate from the rest and don't drown the crayfish by keeping them in too much water.

Even if bait shops in your area carry the bass-tempting morsels, catching your own in the water you're going to fish may still be best. You'll discover color schemes for plug consideration when you run out of the live stuff, and you may come across more soft-shelled specimens.

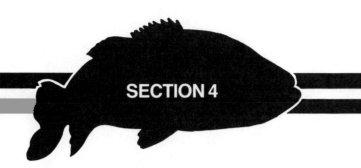

Special Situations

=22=

Pre-Spawn Period

S pawning is not a quick, simple event that occurs each spring. Fingerlings that swim the shallows in the late spring are the result of several months of activity in the life of the bass. The ritual behavior involves various stages for both the male and female. For the purposes of taking a detailed look, we'll define three periods: pre-spawn, spawn (bedding time) and post-spawn. We'll cover pre-spawn bass in this chapter.

The pre-spawn period actually begins in the late fall months. That is when the female bass initiates egg development. It then takes up to four months for the roe mass to fully develop. Large fall-caught bass that are cleaned for the table often have a yellow egg mass in the gestation period.

Bass seem to have a feel for the winter and early spring weather and its influence on their particular environment. It is then that they fulfill their purpose for being. Reproductive instincts, such as the timing of pre-spawn movements and activities, are molded by their own aquatic environment. Inefficient and unproductive traits just can't gain a foothold in the gene pool. As a result the entire spawning process follows a pattern.

Bass in different lakes do not initiate their spawning activities at the same time. Nor do all bass in single, large lakes spawn at the same time. The spawning cycle is just that. It occurs gradually at different times in different climates and at different latitudes. Anglers may find bass in a pre-spawn pattern for a couple of months. They may see bass on beds in different locations over a period of 30 or 45 days.

Such behavior depends on the weather and on the shallows available to the bass. That's particularly true when weather fluctuations are severe and suitable nesting sites are limited. Half of a lake's population of bass may be in a pre-spawn pattern while others are already completing their spawning duties.

The ability of individual fish to participate in the lengthy spawning process is dependent upon its sexual maturity, which is more relative to size than age. Young female bass reach maturity when they are approximately 10 inches long. Males reach maturity when they are 9 inches long. That's normally in the second year of growth for the average bass specimen. Larger bass usually move to shallow waters first and spawn ahead of the smaller females in their clan.

Once fish reach maturity they normally continue to reproduce year after year. Not all mature fish in a population will go through the spawning process. The stress of reproduction is not normally fatal to healthy bass. Bass populations maintain roughly equal numbers of males and females.

Timing And Influences

Pre-spawn behavior and spawning movements to the shallows are dictated by the length of day, the amount of sunlight and the water temperature. The angle of the sun and the sequence of moon cycles are also involved in pre-spawning behavior. This phase is usually in the spring between the months of February and June when the days lengthen.

When the water temperature reaches somewhere between 58 and 62 degrees, most largemouth are in a pre-spawn phase. When the temperature reaches the mid 60s, the majority of females will be hovering over a bed. However, some bass have been found to actually go on the bed in water temperatures as low as 50 degrees. Others have successfully spawned in 75-degree water. The fact remains that the process of spawning takes longer when water temperatures are colder.

Unusually frigid spring weather followed by an abrupt change to unseasonably hot weather can quickly cause elevated water temperatures. Then a female's egg mass may ripen rapidly

Pre-spawn bass move into the shallows from their deep, wintertime haunts. They are healthy, feisty and, at times, very aggressive feeders.

Pre-Spawn Period

and she may drop them all at once in just an hour or two "bedtime." Such hurried efforts are often in old or uncleaned nests or in quickly prepared nests not suitable for a highly successful spawn.

Many researchers believe that the moon phase is related to the initiation of spawning activities. They say the amount of sunlight and sustained temperature are apparently right for the female to drop her eggs around a full moon. The majority of bass do seem to spawn then. Others may spawn on the dark of the moon. In rivers or tidal-influenced waters lunar effects may be negligible. In coastal estuaries the tides are minimal between the full- and new-moon periods. That's the ideal time for brackish-water bass to take on the job. Other environmental factors that affect tidewater fish are level fluctuations of a foot or more and the tide change two to four times each day.

Photoperiod (amount of sunlight) is generally thought to be the most important factor and the key to triggering the spawning process. Photoperiod alone does not determine spring bass locations, but surface temperature is probably more important at this time of year than at any other. Lakes typically have warm pockets of water that may vary 4 or 5 degrees over 300 yards. Such areas are the first to see actual spawning activity.

Weather influences on the spawning process are many. Slowly rising water temperatures are generally optimal for spawning success. Cold fronts drastically influence bass on a bed or disrupt the efforts of those moving in and out of the shallows trying to locate an affable partner and nest. They can also have an adverse effect on the success of the spawn.

Bass trying to move out of the pre-spawn phase to the beds will back away from the shallows to the more comfortable depths when a front arrives. With a slight drop in water temperature, they retreat to their deeper holding areas and may not move back for several days following a warming trend. If weather continues to interrupt the process and the spawn is not successful, the lake's partial or entire year-class can be effectively eliminated. Such results will upset the population balance of that fishery.

Water-level fluctuations can also have drastic effects on a successful spawn. Lakes with erratic springtime water tables have erratic bass production. Drawdowns for irrigation, flood control or other reasons adversely affect not only pre-spawn bass but also the spawning sites and the intended results of that activity. Disoriented bass and abandoned beds mean loss of eggs and a low production for that particular water.

Mature female bass that are not able to spawn are often in a predicament. Some bass in the pre-spawn stage actually skip the spawn and go directly into the post-spawn period. Their egg mass is simply absorbed by the body. Others may develop "roe rot." This means the egg mass hardens during the female's unsuccessful attempt to spawn and the bass eventually dies.

Pre-Spawn Movements

Bass normally start their migration to the flats by way of submerged riverbeds in impoundments and similar types of natural paths in natural lakes. Their movements are governed by their instinctive drive to be in the right place at the right time. The male has to build the nest when conditions dictate and the female's eggs must be developed properly over the course of a specific time period.

If the shallows respond to early warm spells and warm too quickly the female, concerned about early egg development, may remain in the depths. There, cold water will impede premature egg development. Bass tracking studies have shown that during this period the greatest movement occurs in the afternoon. When water temperatures are below 60 degrees individual bass seldom move around at other times of the day.

The two to four weeks just prior to spawning are perhaps the best time of year to catch several large bass. Both sexes are in the best physical shape of the year at that time. Warmer weather has activated some forage life. While competition for food may be severe after the winter months the bass are especially aggressive as they move shallower.

Some of the first movements of the year are geared to bass feeding and bulking up for the rigors of the spawn. Bass may briefly move in and out of shallower water for this purpose. They generally hold on the edge of deep water at first and then move into a shallow area near the spawning grounds a few weeks before going on the beds.

The movements of pre-spawn fish in man-made lakes begin

to evolve around the lake when it's at its coldest. When the temperatures get into the 60s, it's time for the fish to actually move into the nest to spawn. Unlike a small pond, the process in a reservoir takes place at different speeds in different parts of it.

Pre-spawn activity may take place over a two-month time frame. In one part of the lake the fish may move up to get ready for bedding and, when the temperature is correct, go ahead and spawn. In other parts of the lake that warm up more slowly, the fish may still be in a pre-spawn state and receptive to lures.

Staging Locations

In the early spring, smart anglers will search for areas that warm up the quickest and are located adjacent to obvious spawning places. Pre-spawn fish are usually adjacent to areas in which they will eventually spawn. They will then divert to staging areas, temporary gathering points where pre-spawners congregate prior to moving to the spawning flats.

For example, if fish are going to spawn in the back of the pockets they may be staged on the points. You'll want to work the points instead of the back of the pocket because the better fish won't be there for six weeks. They may be in small groups pre-staged on a deeper secondary point if the first ledge off the shallow flat is in very shallow water. When they do start to spawn they will spread out along banks or in the backs of the pockets.

Protected places like the back areas of marinas form jetties and narrow entrances. These are usually good spots to try. Marina basins may have boat ramps, but the shallows are often protected from outside waves. Trees in these areas are frequently nonexistent and the shallows there heat up quicker than other places in the lake. Since protected coves on the north and west banks tend to warm up quicker due to the position of the sun in the southern hemisphere, try fishing those areas first.

During the spring, avoid the middle of the lake with its underwater islands and points leading to deep, open-water areas. Such places are going to remain cold and are the last places pre-spawn bass invade. Fish them late in the spring when other bass are on the beds.

Nice fish, but should you keep pre-spawn bass? Catch-and-release fishing guarantees the future of our sport.

Pre-Spawn Period

Rivers at the headwaters of lakes can provide excellent fishing for pre-spawn bass. They can also be extremely unproductive. If the river has stayed high and flooded over several months with the spring rains, the availability of pre-spawners will depend on whether the showers brought in cold or warm waters. Often such fish will be the last to spawn, due to the instability of the river. Smart bass anglers learn the "timetable" of a particular body of water.

Bass staged on a point, shelf or ledge are easily motivated to move. Unusually warm weather will cause some to go shallow on false spawning runs. They may move up on flats and feed aggressively. When another front hits they move back out to the staging area. Fish are constantly adjusting to the conditions.

The key to catching pre-spawn bass is not in the baits being used but in their presentation and their size. Many anglers like to toss spinnerbaits and crankbaits. If the fish are really tight on cover, they pitch a jig. The tools are often the same. The only difference is the speed with which you work them. Work the lures a little more deliberately and slower than you would under hot-water conditions.

You may want to upgrade the size of your bait. If the lake has a lot of quality fish, use a bigger bait. Even though the bass are not on the nest they are thinking about it, and a bigger bait may trigger more strikes. On the other hand, if the weather becomes severe, the fish may become finicky about hitting the larger fare. Then it's time to downsize the baits.

23

The Spawning Phase

Where bass actually spawn depends on the characteristics of specific waters. Typically, water in the upper end of a reservoir is likely to be warmer than water in the lower end. With the winter sun positioned lower in the southern sky than at other times of the year, those banks on the north side of coves should heat up more quickly. They receive more direct sunlight than the southern shorelines.

Prevailing winds also tend to concentrate spawning bass in specific areas. The wind-free creek shores and leeward cove banks, particularly on the north side, are preferred spots of bedding bass. Areas that attract spawning bass one year will usually do so the following, assuming water levels are the same and vegetation growth is similar.

Both largemouth and smallmouth will usually build their nests in shallow, warmer water on or around some vegetation. In lieu of that, they'll nest on or around rocks, stumps, tree roots or brush. Since the male will have to defend the nest from predators, he'll look for places that lend themselves to such action. If he has only three sides to defend, he won't have such a difficult job.

The selection of a bed site is highly individual and variable. Spawning fish are often concentrated. Males normally select the site. However, they have been known to select a mate first and together cruise the shallows to find a suitable site. The bed

Largemouth bass spawn in shallow, sandy waters adjacent to some form of protective vegetation.

is usually in two to six feet of water to take advantage of the ample sunshine required to help incubate the eggs. Wave action, boating pressure, water clarity, structure and bottom composition each have a bearing on the depth.

Deeper water temperatures can be cooler and bass may spawn later than those bedding in shallower areas. Some bass have been observed spawning in 16 feet of sparsely vegetated, crystal clear water. Due to limited availability of protected bedding sites, it's not unusual to find groups of males building nests along certain shorelines in sheltered bays.

The individual nests are usually spaced several yards apart so that each bass has its own domain.

Male bass, which usually are much smaller than the females, move to the shallows to select nesting sites as the water temperature climbs above 60 degrees. Their thoughts have turned to reproduction and their immediate goal is to locate a good bed site. As the water temperature approaches 65 degrees, they know that the nest should be ready for the ripe female. Once the water reaches that temperature, the female bass has only one more week to carry the eggs before they hatch.

Normally, the male will select the site first and then find a mate. The male also guards the nest once the eggs are laid.

Building The Bed

The male builds the nest by rooting and fanning out a circular depression, usually in a firm, clean bottom. Sand, marl, gravel or rubble on the lake bottom are preferred because the eggs need to adhere to something stable. The nests are usually at least two feet in diameter by six inches deep, but the ultimate size may depend on the size of the female the male gets to join him.

Most of the loose debris is fanned out of the bed area so that the eggs, when laid by the female, won't suffocate. Decaying vegetation uses up oxygen that the eggs will require. If silt covers the eggs once they are dropped onto the nest, they will die.

A light deposit of silt or other sediment that can't be easily fanned away may cause a bass to abandon a bed and find another area for the nest.

Angler traffic can spook a male from the bed, but he'll usually return within five minutes if the angler waits quietly at a reasonable distance. NAFC members can determine what is reasonable based on depth, water clarity and other factors. The male will often pick up and move an angler's lure that has been tossed to the bed. This is especially true after the eggs have been laid and while he is there by himself guarding them.

A lure thrown in the proximity of the nest will often be picked up, carried away and dropped by the male. And if annoyed at any moving object near the bed, he will attack it vigorously. The female, enduring the stress of pregnancy in the nearby staging area, is not as aggressive. The time clock is ticking for both of them.

An angler looking to catch the female at this time may entice a strike by casting toward the deeper water just off the bedding area. The roe-laden female may be positioned very near a heat emitting source, trying to incubate her egg mass. Rocks, posts and other structure near the surface in deeper waters could be providing the extra warmth. She may also be using such structure for a side-rubbing ritual that some underwater observers have noted. This may help to dislodge the eggs and position them better for final ripening.

If the female is on the bed by herself, she may eventually strike a nuisance in the bed such as a lure. While the male is at times easily provoked, the female reacts differently to the presence of an uninvited source of aggravation. She'll softly pick up the fare and blow it out away from the bed.

On The Bed

When the bed is ready, the courting male repeatedly swims out to slightly deeper water in search of an eligible female to lead her back to the nest. If the parent-to-be is reluctant to take the pre-nuptial cruise, the aggressive male will even force the usually much larger female to his bed. He will batter and butt the female with his nose to guide her to the right bed, which may lie among several in a spawning flat.

The pair then slowly circle the bed. The female may even finish fanning the nest with her tail. The male continues his physical contact by nipping and pushing at her side and belly until she is ready. They move to their positions over the bed. This normally occurs during low-light times. They are side by side, tilted vertically to assure that their vents are near. The male exhibits vivid and rapid color pattern changes.

While the female rests and floats above the nest, she ejects the eggs at intervals as they ripen in her ovaries. The eggs sink slowly into the nest. The male must remain close by to fertilize them with milt. He usually does that when the female is finished by ejecting milt over the egg mass and then moving his tail back and forth to assure that all are fertilized.

The egg-dropping activity is accompanied by spasms of the female's body. The deposited eggs in the nest have soft, adhesive surfaces. They adhere to the brush, roots and weeds in the nest.

The size of the female usually determines the number of eggs she is capable of depositing. Many experts believe that a bass lays up to 5,000 eggs per pound of body weight. A 4- or 5-pound bass is considered the most successful spawner in terms of egg viability. She may drop 4,000 to 6,000 eggs every two weeks over a six-week period, and she may drop eggs in more than one nest.

When through, the physically debilitated female has then laid from 5,000 to 20,000 eggs in the male's nest. A large fish may only have laid a portion of the egg mass she was carrying. She may withhold eggs instinctively during unstable weather for another attempt days or weeks later. Once her role is finished and the male has fertilized all the eggs, the female usually deserts the nest. One will occasionally hang around a day or so to help guard the nest.

If the female is reluctant to leave, the male normally drives her away. He quickly comes back to fan the eggs in the bed with his tail. It is not unusual for him to go out and seek another female, or even two, to add egg mass to his clan. If successful, the male could have up to 40,000 offspring to protect.

Fanning the eggs oxygenates them and helps remove gasses that the egg mass may produce while maturing. Male bass are extremely intent during this period and may even fan their tails ragged. Males with bloody tails are not unusual during the spawn. While it is believed that the success of the spawn is dependent upon the water circulation furnished by the male, many well-guarded nests have developed fungus infections and have been lost. Bass eggs left unattended have been hatched in laboratory facilities.

A second part of the male's workload after the eggs have

Bass that are spawning are not interested in feeding, but they are protective of any intrusions into their nest area. Big bass caught at this time of year should be released to carry out their reproductive chores.

been laid is to stand guard as the sole protector. A male guarding the nest won't eat but will fend off each egg predator. He'll chase off one attacker after another. Small predatory fish like bluegill or shiners just wait for the male bass to drop his guard or leave the nest, providing an opportunity for the attacker to raid the bed and gorge itself on eggs.

Bluegill constantly circle the nest and use wolf-pack tactics to work a bass bed. One will try to distract the bass by darting in to gobble eggs and draw his chase. Another will slip in from behind to eat some eggs quickly and leave. While the male is still on the spawning flats battling panfish he is very susceptible to being caught.

In three to nine days the eggs hatch, and swarms of fry hover over the nest while absorbing their life-sustaining yolk sacs. A sudden drop in water temperature delays hatching time and may even kill the eggs. Most usually survive and some eggs carried in the nest for as long as two weeks have hatched successfully.

The yolk sac is gone within a week. One week later a tiny tail develops, allowing the newborn to swim. It is at this time that the male, having gone mostly without food for a few weeks, reportedly devours some of his young fry. He may swallow a third of them, stopping only when they have scattered. In what may be nature's way of alerting the young to the predatory relationships they will be facing, the male ravages the brood.

Leaving The Bed

Survivors of that ritual, now about an inch in length, move to the shallow, more protected shoreline. Plankton and tiny crustaceans are the principal foods for bass under 2 inches. Aquatic and terrestrial insects, especially in nymph and larvae stages, become important ingredients in a bass' diet four to six weeks after the spawn. A bass can ingest amazing numbers of mosquito larvae at this time. But it is at the 1-inch stage that the spawn success can again be affected. Scarcity of plankton food supplies when feeding begins will quickly deplete the young bass population.

The male leaves the bed following the spawn. Another male often moves in to recondition the bed for its mate. As one group of spawners moves into post-spawn activity, another group may be staged and ready to move in and take its place.

After the spawning ritual, both the male and female bass are energy-depleted. The female may remain immobile in deeper water for several hours. She is weak from the trauma of egg laying and not easily able to exert further energy. Neither will actively pursue forage or anglers' lures.

If your favorite lake has a bay with a channel in it, the flat area or shoreside nearest that channel may hold the most bass. Females will come up and spawn and then move back into the channel. They may stay right at that point for a day or two. They eventually work deeper down the channel to the main staging area where they'll remain for a couple of weeks to recoup from the rigors of the spawn.

When the spawn is completed by all females in a lake, 50,000 tiny bass may surface. No lake could support such a population so predation and other factors reduce the count over the following four months to around 200 fingerling-size bass per acre. Survivors then change from a diet of plankton and grass shrimp to small minnows and their runty brethren. When they reach maturity only 5 to 10 percent of the 200 minnows per acre will remain.

Less than one percent of the eggs actually develop into catchable-size bass, but I believe in giving the fishery as much opportunity as possible to flourish. I don't think we have to disturb bass on the beds to enjoy catch-and-release fishing. There are plenty of pre-spawn or post-spawn fish to lure to your baits.

But once males and females have recuperated from the rigors of the spawn, that's a different story, as we will see in our next chapter.

24

Post-Spawn Period

North American Fishing Club members and other anglers will normally find bass in post-spawn movements when water temperatures are around 70 degrees. The bass have just dispersed to deeper areas as their fingerlings scatter to the shallows. One of the first signs this has happened is that shallow-water activity has waned. Post-spawn bass don't all behave the same way. They don't leave the beds at the same time, nor do they migrate in one mass toward their summer holes. Catching after-spawn fish is not easy.

During the entire spawning process the sex of the bass plays a part in its feeding and striking habits. Male bass, which seldom feed during the spawning period, are usually more susceptible to capture when they are guarding the nest than after their duties are completed. After the spawn fishing can get tough.

While they are building nests, males try to keep any invaders away and are very protective against any potential egg-eating predator. Male bass are on the lookout for bluegill, salamanders, crayfish and certain minnow species. A lure crawled through their bed may trigger a protective reaction, a non-feeding response. They have no such incentive right after the spawn.

Pre-spawn females lying in deep water show little interest in feeding, as baitfish move freely among the ripe sows without apprehension. The bedding female may be coaxed into picking up a nuisance bait if the male is not around. Females may occasionally feed while on the bed but reportedly take only what appears to be injured forage.

In a post-spawn condition, females won't spend much energy chasing anything. They'll simply suck in a bait gently to check out its edibility. After spawning, the big females may be hungry but they're physically spent. Tempting baitfish can swim among the lethargic bass again without much fear. The female will regain full strength after a couple of weeks. Then all forage fish and fingerling bass beware!

After leaving the bed a post-spawn transition rapidly occurs for the parents. This may be the toughest fishing period of the year. The male bass will guard the fry as they swim up from the nest and then off to their own demise. He then will usually move off and linger in the shallows to feed since he hasn't been eating much while on guard duty. There's more food available in the shallows so the males will stay in the spawning flats area before dropping back to their summer homes in deeper water.

The females have quickly dropped back to deep, open-water areas. They appear lethargic from the rigors of the spawn. They may be dormant for up to two weeks. Few females are caught during this recuperation period and the fact that they have relocated probably plays a larger part than many anglers believe. Those females that are taken probably are in their pre-spawn or spawn phase.

"I think that if you could dive down and see them, the females would be lying on the bottom," notes former biologist Bob Knopf. "It would be like they were recovering from surgery. The males go through the same thing but are not affected as severely. They're not quite as tough to catch.

"Catching the females, even when you're right on them, is often impossible," he continues. "They are so inactive during the post-spawn period you have to concentrate on the males if you hope to catch any fish."

As their normal bodily functions return and the warming waters pump up their metabolic rate, the females begin to feed. That's when they are once again susceptible to an angler's lure, albeit a more deeply presented one.

Post-spawn bass are weak and are interested in recuperating from the spawning process, but they will hit slow-moving lures.

Post-Spawn Period   219

Post-Spawn Location/Relocation

The larger bass have moved deeper. They are the first to spawn and vacate the area. Only smaller bass remain in the shallow spawning flats to take advantage of the numerous spring hatches. Bluegill and other prime forage fish spawn in the same general area a few weeks after the bass, usually when the water temperature hits 70 degrees. To catch the big fish you'll have to go to more summer-like patterns. Remember that those particular fish are in a post-spawn period.

You could simply relocate. The best way to combat the post-spawn doldrums is to either move from one cove to another on the opposite shore or to change from a shallow body of water to a deeper one where the fish spawn may not have reached the post-spawn period. Spawning phases overlap on all large waters.

You can actually move from a post-spawn area to a spawn area on the same lake. If you do this over the course of a couple of weeks you should find that the post-spawn bass you came across early on have now recovered and are in a more active state.

Different spawning areas in the same lake often peak at different times. If it's protected from the north wind a spawning area might peak early. If the area is not sheltered, the bass may spawn there a month later than those at the other spot. It's best to find where the bass have spawned most recently since there will be more bass still in that area.

Bass in the highly protected areas in the backs of creeks have a tendency to spawn earlier and move out more quickly than others. Other bass may stay shallow for about a month after coming off the bed. Some may be lethargic while others may go on aggressive feeding forays.

The fish are physically drained but they may feed heavily to regain their strength. The spawning process may go on for a couple of months and the male may spawn with two or three different females. He'll be tired and the females are even more tired and harder to catch. After the spawn it may be four to six weeks before the bass are again easily patterned.

Specific Areas And Structures

In some lakes post-spawn bass move off to deep water and

suspend. An angler can't catch many of them for two months or so during the post-spawn phase since these fish don't school in shallow water to feed. Shallower lakes often don't experience this super slow, post-spawn period. Bass there may scatter in four to 10 feet of highly vegetated water and along the shallow sides of points. They will stay close to the spawning grounds at the shallower side of that range in dingy water and deeper in clear. Fishing success is normally better in stained conditions at this time of year.

Many post-spawn bass then move to mid-depth water (six to 12 feet) on nearby points and creek beds along their main route of migration away from the spawning flats. These are their initial pre-summer feeding stations. Finding them during this period may be difficult. If you do locate the fish, you could be in for several rod bends because they tend to rejoin their schools.

The bass will usually abandon the shallow shores where they were tightly concentrated. They'll move first to the immediate points in a cove, then on to the outside points and finally to the main points of the lake. Dense vegetation in deeper water not far from a spawning site may delay them.

While the prime pre-spawn condition for the angler may be clear water, post-spawn fishing conditions are ideal when the water is stained. Add to that choppy water, a rising barometer and overcast sky, and the time is right to find and catch some largemouth. Rising water, not falling, helps to activate some of the fish and make them more aggressive.

The angler must follow the rapid transition and the bass migration down the tributary or lake from the shallows. Prime mid-depth structures are long sloping points, ditches, shallow rock piles or ledges and roadbeds that lead to deep water. Most mature bass have now vacated the spawning flats not to return until next spring.

Shallow Luring Success

Most anglers will want to start out after the spawn using small lures and then switch to progressively larger baits toward the end of the post-spawn period. In-line, or straight-shaft, spinners are effective baits as the bass leave their beds. Small spoons and minnow baits fool those bass insistent on hanging around shallow areas for a few weeks.

Strikes are once again triggered by hunger and reflex action. The lure's edibility again takes on paramount importance. It must smell, feel and look alive in its movements to attract post-spawn bass. The spawn is over and the bass' senses are primed for foraging and getting on with their growth.

Surface lures are often productive for post-spawn largemouth, particularly when fished early or late in the day and on partly cloudy days. Retrieve them slowly around the bass fry, which are usually near the shallow spawning beds. Let the plug sit motionless once it has landed. You have to slow down the presentation to get them to bite.

Review maps and pinpoint the best spawning areas, those flats with nearby deep-water access. If you find a lot of fry in an area, the bass will usually be in nearby cover. Try tossing a spinnerbait or buzzbait to check out the area. You may not attract one of the non-aggressive bass to chase the lure but you might see the fry. Then, pick up a minnow plug and fish it slowly on top.

Deeper/Tighter Offerings

Some experienced guides opt for plastic worms with light sinkers when post-spawn bass are located in mid-depth waters along points or drops. They'll fan-cast such spots. If the structure extends for several feet in one direction at the same depth, the angler should cast parallel to it. The front ends of boat houses, rock ledges or submerged creek banks are examples of areas where this approach can be very effective.

Post-spawn bass that start relating to the inner edges of existing grassbeds in a lake require a different approach. Changes, such as points and pockets along the edge, attract the fish. The bass will be on waters with stumps or logs. It will be more difficult, however, to tempt them.

Flippin' and pitchin' are also effective techniques for these post-spawn bass. Plastic worms and lizards are still excellent baits when the bass are suspended off the edges of ridges. Bass tend to be non-aggressive when suspended. They will often become more aggressive when a plastic lizard or waterdog imitation invades their territory at this time of year. A ⅜-ounce jig and frog-shaped Berkley Strike Rind is a good combination pitchin' bait, particularly for a lunker.

Slightly deeper and darker spots attract bass after the spawn. Within a couple of weeks some of the post-spawn fish will go on a feeding binge.

Post-Spawn Period   223

A vibrating bait can cover a lot of water when you're searching for an aggressive group of bass. While you may miss a lot of fish when throwing a Rat-L-Trap or Hot Spot at this time of year, remember that you are hunting only the bass that are biting. Cast the lure. Allow it to sink completely to the bottom and then reel back. This high-speed technique can be very effective on post-spawn fish only if you cover a lot of water.

Crayfish-like lures are usually effective in the spring as live crustaceans are digging out of their winter holes. The soft plastic versions, as well as deep-running crankbait imitations, are productive for post-spawn bass. Add a little fish attractant, which provides the artificial a fish slime, and you have a powerful and effective weapon.

Crankbaits should be retrieved to make contact with the cover in which the bass are holding. The reel, bump and pause method can be successful for those anglers with a good sense of feel. The majority of strikes will occur as the buoyancy of the bait floats it upward from the structure. The angler has to be ready to notice the soft tap and respond.

As the post-spawn period comes to an end, the bass begin to school and so do the fishermen.

25

Water Level Changes

Sudden drawdowns that force a lake's water level to drop rapidly will cause bass to back off into deeper water where anglers have difficulty finding them, says well-known pro fisherman Tommy Martin.

"A drop of six inches within a week has a significant bearing on the location of the fish," he says. "This is especially true in the spring when the bass are first moving up to spawn.

"In the east Texas lakes, like Toledo Bend and Sam Rayburn, hydrilla can be found in six- to 15-foot depths during the spring," explains Martin. "We often have a seven- or eight-inch drop during the week that will move the bass. They will back out of the bushes and into the deeper hydrilla to spawn."

Martin marks the water level on a tree in any lake that he is going to fish for several days. He can then return to the same tree and note what change has taken place.

Knowing the level fluctuation during the off-limits period of a tournament may possibly provide information on the whereabouts of bass located in pretournament practice. He'll always mark the lake's level during practice and return two or three weeks later for the tournament.

The Corps of Engineers, or other responsible water management authority, also can be consulted for lake level information. When he is unable to practice on a lake before a tournament, Martin will call them a month before an event and record the reading and date. He will then call them the day before the official practice starts and evaluate the difference.

"They'll generally tell you if they are going to be generating power and dropping the lake or whether they are going to hold the lake level steady," Martin says. "They're pretty good about telling you what you want to know. If you have to adjust to a rapid drop, you can be prepared."

Edge Movements

When water depths are reduced, fish that were up in the shallow bushes will just drop off into the creeks next to 10 to 13 feet of water. Most of the reservoirs, even those without submerged vegetation such as hydrilla, have well-defined creek channels within the coves where the water may drop from five to 15 feet. The bass sense that the water is falling and they stay close to the edges of the channels.

When the lake starts falling the shad react similarly to the bass by moving out of the very shallow water to the deeper water. On most of the east Texas lakes in the fall, the big schools of threadfin will stay in 30 or 40 feet of water once the level begins to drop. A calm lake in the fall will probably show signs of many shad schools on the surface just before dusk.

When the lake is falling Martin searches for more vertical banks where the lake bottom quickly drops into the depths.

"On the east Texas lakes, we really don't fish right up on the banks that much," he explains. "We'll fish back in the bushes that are near the bank, the flooded willows and the flooded buck bushes—places like that. Still, the majority of the fish are caught in the outer bushes, the ones farthest out in the lake, because they are near deeper water.

"The bigger bass are usually out there, even in the spring," says Martin. "The big ones won't go way back into the shallow bushes in one or two foot of water. They'll stay out in three to five feet of water next to 10 or 15 feet of water. That's where they'll spawn."

Post-Spawn Effects

In the post-spawn period when the majority of the bass have finished bedding, a falling lake will have less effect on the fish. A rapid drop may still move some fish, though. In the summer, for example, the hydrilla can be found growing in 23 feet of water on Sam Rayburn, and during a big water level change, the shallow bass may move into it.

Martin feels that if the waters only fall six inches or so over a three-week period, most bass will not be affected. Largemouth on the extremely flat banks would most probably be the exception.

Even in very shallow water, bass on the steeper banks will be less affected by a drop during the post-spawn period. Bushes in four to six feet of water with deep water running up to the bank are excellent spots to fish in the spring when the water is falling, according to Martin.

"A lot of bass will move to their summer pattern as the water temperature rises above 75 degrees. Out in the deep hydrilla, those fish generally won't be affected too much by a falling lake," Martin adds. "During the early part of the summer they'll move out to the drops on the deep grasslines where the creek channels cut through the grass. When they move to the outer ridges in 15- to 20-foot depths with grass and 30 feet of water all around them, those fish are not affected."

Lakes generally drop the most during the late summer and fall, according to Martin. Rainfall is minimal and the power generation at each dam takes its toll on the water supply in many lakes. Water evaporation, electricity use and irrigation all have an effect on water levels then.

Falling Fall

"In the east Texas lakes we usually see a rapid drop in elevation during August, September and October," says Martin. "Then we go to the deep hydrilla lines out on the ridges in the middle of the lake. A hydrilla bed that is in 15 to 18 feet of water on the edge and drops off into water 20 and 30 feet deep is what we look for."

The fish on the flat lakes in east Texas seldom relate to the banks in the fall, according to Martin. They stay out in the deeper water among the vegetation. Spinnerbaits fished over the grass in seven or eight feet of water are effective on the relatively shallow bass then. The best procedure is fishing heavy baits down on the deeper grass.

On lakes without milfoil or hydrilla the bass will relate to

Tommy Martin derives success on many lakes by analyzing the water level fluctuations. Knowing how such changes affect bass movement is a key to fishing productivity.

the banks during the fall. Bass will inhabit the shoreline cover such as stumps and rocks. However, when the water is dropping most will be near the steeper banks rather than the flat banks.

Martin fishes a lot of lakes in the fall when a quick drop in water may push bass off the creek channel banks. His most memorable experience occurred on Joe Wheeler Reservoir in northern Alabama. He won the 1974 B.A.S.S. Masters Classic under conditions that left most contenders wondering how he did it.

"It was late October and the lake was falling rapidly," recounts Martin. "We had been told that the waters had been falling for quite some time and that the fish weren't hitting."

When he found out that the reservoir had been dropping so quickly he established his game plan. On the first day of practice he fished stumps and bushes in shallow, flat water for three hours. His catch of skinny, 12- and 13-inch bass from the two- to three-foot water helped eliminate those areas.

Steep Channel Drops

Martin then moved out to steeper, vertical banks where creek channels with 10 to 15 feet of water were in close proximity. Large chunk rock and isolated stumps made the place ideal. He started catching 2- to 4-pound bass from the cover.

Looking for channel banks became a priority for Martin. He fished more vertical, steeper banks with channels nearby. Most of the other fishermen were fishing visible cover out on the flats in very shallow water. They were catching only little fish.

Deep, winter fish don't even know the lake is falling, Martin surmises. Bass in 35 or 40 feet of water are not affected at all then. They are not going anywhere, according to the guide. The shallow fish are affected by the rapid drawdown.

On most flatland lakes the water level isn't drawn down rapidly enough to create a current. Mountain lakes in Alabama, Georgia and Virginia do experience a visible movement of water. Fishing a current like this requires an adjustment in strategy.

"I was tossing a worm on Lake Moultrie in South Carolina near where the canal comes into the lake," relates Martin. "The water was really flowing, and I was fishing a sandbar with some difficulty. The current was sweeping the worm by quickly and it was hard to detect the strikes.

"I was trying to feel the worm in the current and all of a sudden I would realize that the bass had it and I'd catch one," he says. "I missed about a dozen bass there that day because it was hard to fish the strong current. I was fishing a slip-sinker rig but should have probably been using an exposed hook rig."

Martin, using his electric motor, was holding his boat in the current and casting against the current to the sandbar. He placed his boat on the backside of the sandbar where an eddy was formed. As his offering was washed off the bar into the eddy, bass would strike. Although he missed several hits, the professional did catch a heavy limit that day.

"You can find that situation one day and go back the next and there will be hardly any current," adds Martin. "You might find a strong current and go back just two hours later and find none."

A good bass angler pays attention to quick changes in conditions and adjusts to them rapidly to stay on the fish. While drawdowns are a man-made challenge, natural ones like the wind can also be perplexing for NAFC bass fishermen.

=====26=====

Wind Strengths

igh winds have been known to disrupt established patterns. They are consistently responsible for bass movement, rough boating conditions and angler frustration. Any North American Fishing Club member who has been challenged by heavy winds knows exactly what I'm talking about when I call these gales disruptive.

Not everyone hates the wind, though. Many professional fishermen have learned to extract their bounty from the teeth of a gale. I talked to many of them when gathering information for this book for NAFC members.

For example, during four days of extremely high winds, Ken Cook won Super B.A.S.S. I on Florida's St. Johns River. He attributes his success on windblown waters there and elsewhere to the wave action stirring up sediments and food sources for small organisms.

"Bass are drawn to the area for the food," says Cook. "They can feed there with confidence because of the 'cover' of waves and/or muddied water. Over the years I've noticed that bass on exposed banks seem to be turned on by wind and wave action."

Fellow pro fisherman Ron Shearer agrees.

"The wind is a good thing," he says. "It's a lot easier to catch fish with some wind blowing across an area than with none."

George Cochran also believes that wind on a big lake is a

significant factor. This angler who is most familiar with the wide Arkansas River contends that wind makes the bass fishing better if you know what to look for at a particular time of year. Whitecaps are not foreign to many tournament sites that Cochran and other touring pros have visited.

Anchor Dragging

Bass waters don't come any larger than Lake Okeechobee in southern Florida where the wind velocity can increase quickly. Shearer was undaunted by spring gales during one invitational tournament held there.

"I managed to catch a limit of bass in the tournament that day when the wind happened to come up on us," he explains. "I dragged four anchors and the boat was still moving fast through the area. The fish were there, though. And I knew it."

Shearer's effective technique was simple. He threw the worm out as far as he could in front of the boat. While drifting toward the bait he reeled up the slack and set the hook hard when he got a strike.

The Hardin, Kentucky, pro admits that it is very difficult to hold the boat in high winds in order to catch bass. Shearer has found, though, that it is possible to pull a lot of fish from the windblown environment. Dragging two or three anchors and flippin' the grassbeds in natural lakes has been a very productive technique for him.

"To be successful at this type of fishing you have to know where the bass are beforehand," stresses Shearer. "There's no way you can effectively find bass in this type cover with a high wind blowing."

Baitfish Collection

Larry Williams feels that water movement holds the key to effectively catch windblown bass. In such weather conditions, he'll be on the lookout for places that may collect baitfish.

A cut into a creek from a shallow bay is an ideal spot during high winds. The northern bassman believes that although you can toss most lure types and catch fish from the cuts, you must bring it out with the current.

"The wind will blow water into a large bay, which will create a current washing out of the cut into the channel," says

High winds make it difficult to control your cast or even fish effectively, but they do turn big bass on.

Wind Strengths

Williams. "These areas are better if the current is washing out of shallows since they usually possess a higher food content."

The pro likes to fish bridge areas, seawall breaks and even culverts with the wind blowing into them. He advises not to be afraid of fishing the windy shorelines and points. Williams prefers lures that most closely imitate the baitfish that are being blown up on the banks. That's what the bass are accustomed to seeing during this foraging.

Tommy Martin chooses between spinnerbaits, crankbaits and buzzbaits when fishing during high winds. Worms or jigs require feel and Martin is aware of the difficulty in detecting strikes during high winds. The wind and wave action usually make the bass more active, according to the Texan.

Windy flats with underwater vegetation such as hydrilla or milfoil can be good, according to Martin. Rocky points or points with underwater stumps are also good places to catch bass when the wind is blowing in on them. He looks for riprap, underwater shoals or small humps out in the lake during high winds. The key element on the topography must be cover of some type.

"Small pockets or coves just off the main lake are good when the wind is blowing into them. The wind blows plankton into these areas and the shad feed on the plankton," he adds. "The wind makes the bass in that area active and they feed on the shad. They'll chase lures well, too!"

Tight-Line Lures

Ken Cook's lure selection in high winds is also well-defined. In windy weather he fishes with the more practical, tight-line lures such as spinnerbaits or crankbaits. When casting drop baits such as worms or jigs into the wind, he says difficulties can arise.

"My favorite is spinnerbaits but the lure choice should be dictated by cover type more than by any other single thing," says Cook. "I use spinnerbaits in weeds, reeds, moss, brush and trees to minimize hangups. If the bank is fairly obstruction-free, I'll more likely use a crankbait that matches the size and type of available food."

Cook will fish all points with a little bit of current to help position feeding fish. And he'll be on the windy banks, regardless of how rough it is. How windy is too windy to fish those spots? According to Cook, it's "when the boat sinks."

Cochran determines which points to fish during high winds by the time of year. In the spring the fish will be in the coves. The wind will pull the bass out onto the points and windy banks in the cove.

"The bass will be in dingier water just behind the points looking for baitfish," says Cochran. "Sometimes they're in the calm water just out of the wind. And in the summer they are on the main lake points and dingy banks."

Clarity Considerations

Shearer notes that waters that are extremely clear require special consideration. The best factor for fishing in the wind, according to the burly pro, is finding a windblown shoreline, especially on a clear lake. The shore is being stirred up and a mud ring develops.

"Once the muddy water appears, that signals bass that forage are being washed out of rocks," says Shearer. "Hence, a jig or crayfish-colored crankbait is very effective."

Fishing the sides of points in a high wind is also an extremely good pattern for him. The wind sets up a lot of current around the points and a mud ring, caused by this turbulence, is often pushed along.

"Bass will hold behind these points and move up in the low visibility waters to feed," says Shearer. "They will usually go around the point and feed just off the breakers. That is an excellent jig or crankbait pattern."

When the wind direction is perpendicular to a bridge the current is forced through the pilings. Forage is then washed through the bridge area, which attracts the bass—and Shearer. Wind will blow schools of shad around and wash crayfish out of shoreline rocks. This is one more reason Shearer is extremely partial to a good wind.

"About the only exception is in the spring when I'm fishing cold, muddy water. That's the worst time to try to catch fish and I certainly don't want a wind then," says Shearer. "I want it to be still so that the shallow water is allowed to warm up quicker. Once the water warms the baitfish will become active, and so will the bass."

Jerk And Hook

On extremely clear waters buffeted by high winds, Larry Williams relies on a jerk technique to fool bass. A bright sun makes his method of fishing large Rapalas over wide, three- to eight-foot-deep flats even more deadly.

"When I say jerk, I mean jerk it as hard as you can," says Williams. "I'll jerk the Rapala for perhaps 10 to 15 feet and then suddenly stop it. Then, just wiggle your rodtip for a second. This will generally get you the strike. If not, start jerking and stop it again."

Williams prefers the larger Rapalas. By drifting with the wind and throwing downwind with a spinning rod and 10-pound test, he can cast an amazing distance even with the Rapala. The Yankee basser can cover a lot of area in a short time.

"If you stop and think about it, it's an area that very few people are fishing," explains Williams. "Most people are either fishing the bank or out on the sharp drop-off on one extremity of the flat."

The professionals are often faced with high winds during the course of several consecutive tournament days on the water. Many have learned to adapt to windy conditions that would normally drive the rest of us off the water. They have had to, though. Money was on the line. NAFC members can learn from the hard work and experience of these pros.

Another natural variant, temperature, can have a powerful impact on bass fishing, and the pros can teach us a few things there, too. It's sure a lot easier to improve our skills and increase our fishing fun that way so greater success can come more quickly.

27

Cold Fronts

S table weather often motivates bass to be in a cooperative mood. Decreasing water pH in the fall allows them to move into the shallows and remain there until cold weather arrives.

The first cold front of the winter, if severe, may be a shock to bass unprepared for the occurrence. Slight thermal variations have lulled them into complacency. They are still inhabiting gentle sloping flats and shallow cover. They can turn on to the cooling effect or abruptly lose interest in foraging after the front moves through. That makes fishing conditions tougher.

George Cochran, Larry Nixon, Woo Daves and Rick Clunn are exposed to such conditions during the course of their average 200 days on the water each year. Sooner or later each will have to figure out a productive fall or winter pattern for catching a few largemouth just after the season's initial cold front.

George Cochran fishes tournaments throughout the country as well as those near his home in North Little Rock, Arkansas. He spends enough days on the water to be very familiar with cold fronts. He says the first one of each year is like many others that follow.

"When you are catching fish in a particular area in the late fall and the weather gets bad, that's cause for concern," says Cochran. "You are not able to catch fish as easily.

"What it does is put the fish into the cover," he explains.

The author feels that lure selection is critical depending on the timing of the cold front. He'll pick a vibrating bait initially and go to a worm or jig when the bass move inside cover.

"About the only way to catch bass then is to flip in the bushes. If you begin to catch them in heavy cover move in on it."

Cochran recommends fishing slower with worms and jigs after the front. He'll also stay longer in one place, working it thoroughly. He says the negative effects of that first, harsh cold front on angling success can be reduced by moving in tighter on cover as the bass do.

Larry Nixon has met with great success on several tournament trails and has often faced frontal conditions to become one of the country's best all-around bass anglers.

"The first cold front usually triggers bass to start the fall feeding frenzy," says Nixon. "It starts the water temperature dropping to a more comfortable range. I fish whatever cover a lake has to offer, and this time of year bass are relocating close to deeper water."

On windy days after a front, he likes to use spinnerbaits or crankbaits. Nixon says the bass are normally very active early in the fall and your lures should likewise be active.

He has discovered that after the front has passed and the wind dies, fish will usually go inside the cover. He says they are then hard to catch, and flippin' a jig or worm into the heart of the cover may be the only thing that will work.

"Still, an angler must remember the main consideration in locating bass and that is cover or structure," Nixon stresses. "If there is a shortage of shallow cover they have to be on some type of offshore structure. Crankbaits work well there to locate key feeding spots.

"A good front sometimes will put a school of fish on these deeper holes," says Nixon. "Spoons, worms, jigs and grubs produce well once you locate such a honey hole."

Two Types Of Fronts

Woo Daves, from Chester, Virginia, who does well in top money tournaments around the country, says he usually sees two types of cold fronts during a year.

"The first is in the spring when you have had warm weather for a period of time," he says. "And as surely as there is a tournament, there will be a drop in temperature the day before. The second type of cold front is in the fall when the temperature seems to drop overnight.

"In the fall, usually you start having mild temperature drops," he says. "Then all of a sudden you get the major drop and the fishing action seems to taper off."

Whether it's a spring or fall cold front, Daves says the same techniques apply.

"You have to slow down at first," he advises. "This is sometimes hard to do, but you have to mentally prepare yourself. When you have been used to fishing at high speed and a bad front drops in, you have to adjust immediately.

"The first rule after a severe cold front hits is to slow the lure down," says Daves. "The second rule is to slow it down some more. And the third rule is to slow it even more! Now you're getting close to retrieving a lure slow enough."

After a front moves through your area, the fish seem to hold tight to cover and it is ever so important to work structure thoroughly, closely and slowly. You have to present your lure just about on the bass' nose to get him to strike, according to Daves. Bass won't move far to take a lure. That's one reason a flipper seems to really excel during cold front conditions. It's probably the best technique to work an area thoroughly.

When fishing severe cold front conditions, Daves will use the flipping method 80 percent of the time. He'll work a jig or worm down deep in the cover close to the logs, brush piles and the like. This has been more productive than any other method for him.

Recorder Magic

"The second pattern in cold front conditions is to turn your graph on and start looking for drops," Daves says. "Fish are generally not in a feeding mood during a bad cold front and will hold right on drops or ledges. I will fish these areas with a crankbait, crank it down fast to get the depth and then slow it down to a crawl. If this doesn't work I will fish a jig and pig or spinnerbait very slowly."

When fishing structure on drop-offs during a cold front, Daves will select a longer rod than normal and lighter line, sometimes 8-pound test, to get the lure down deeper. If a crankbait gets down a little deeper that allows the angler to work it a little slower.

"Another very important thing to remember," says Daves,

Rick Clunn often switches to jigs during cold front conditions. He flips them into shallow cover away from creek channels.

Cold Fronts

"is concentration. During severe cold front conditions it is more important than at any other time. You have to face the reality that you and everyone else are going to get fewer bites than under normal conditions. You must make each one count. Remember, many tournaments at that time of year are won with two fish."

Positive/Negative Effects

Rick Clunn, three-time B.A.S.S. Classic champion, is himself a study in concentration. His ability to dedicate every movement toward catching bass is well-known. Being able to adjust to cold fronts is definitely among his capabilities.

"The first cold front of the fall actually has a positive effect on fishing," says Clunn. "Its cooling effect on the water and its signaling of the oncoming winter actually cause the fish to become much more aggressive and active about feeding."

The bass professional feels that the only possible deterrent to the activity might be excessive wind. That wouldn't hurt the fishing, only hinder an angler's ability to fish, according to Clunn. He has found that bass will group more after the front. The reduced fall fishing pressure, due to those anglers that hunt or watch sports on TV, has an added positive effect on his ability to concentrate on post-frontal fishing at this time of year.

The rear one-third areas of major creeks and coves are Clunn's favorite places to fish in the fall. Those areas are prime for tossing small crankbaits and spinnerbaits of various sizes. He prefers to use a crankbait along the old creek channels in depths ranging from one to eight feet.

Clunn switches to a spinnerbait where the cover gets thicker and also to fish shallow cover away from the creek channel. His third alternative is flipping a 5/16-ounce jig into the thickest cover along a shallow channel when the front is a particularly bad one.

When the weather conditions are constant you can figure out the bass and go out and catch them the same way day after day. But when a front is approaching you have to closely monitor the weather and hope that the bass will open their mouths.

28

Water Chemistry Factors

N orth American Fishing Club members who understand water chemistry, along with the effects of other natural occurrences we've already covered, will have the greatest success at consistently catching more bass. When you know how it affects bass, you can use water chemistry to adjust your techniques. For example, Ken Cook recognized the prime early morning pattern and a different, more productive technique for later in the day to win a bass tournament on Lake Granbury in Texas. His knowledge of how water chemistry affects bass behavior and movements helped him weigh in impressive limits of largemouth. His win there is a prime example of the value of knowing water parameters such as clarity, temperature, pH and oxygen levels and their effect upon largemouth bass.

"I found fishing a topwater lure around boat docks in clear water during morning hours and then pitching a spinnerbait in shallow, muddier water in the afternoon to be productive," says the professional angler. "Combining these two patterns allowed me to be fishing the most active fish in the lake all day.

"The fish in clear water retreated from the structure," Cook explains. "They would suspend over deep water during midday and were difficult to catch. The fish in the shallow, muddier water were not as drastically affected because of less photosynthesis from a lower population level of phytoplankton.

"Fishermen are being bombarded with new data about how

to use water characteristics to find bass," notes the former fisheries biologist. "I get asked about it a lot."

Cook says it's easier today than ever before to determine the appropriate water parameters and understand how they affect the catch. New technology offers simple-to-use instruments that measure pH, temperature and clarity at any depth. Fishermen are now able to understand bass more like fisheries biologists.

After graduating from Oklahoma State University with a fisheries management degree in 1969, Cook worked as a fisheries biologist for the Oklahoma Department of Wildlife and Conservation for 13 years. He spent many hours on the water obtaining data on the fishery and water chemistry. From the studies Cook was able to form definite concepts regarding the bass/water parameter relationships, and he's willing to share those insights here to help North American Fishing Club members.

He used those ideas successfully in a handful of major fishing tournaments before turning full-time to professional bass fishing in 1982. Thanks to his fisheries background, the fisherman from the tiny mining town of Meers, Oklahoma, has few equals in the sport. He often shares his knowledge about bass species and how to catch them at almost-weekly public appearances and seminars around the country. When a bass fisheries biologist talks, the smart fishermen will listen.

"Measurement of pH is probably the single most important chemical characteristic of water affecting fish activity," he boldly states. "Water clarity is second and oxygen is probably third."

Cook says all those factors are very closely tied to the sun. And it is the sun that has the greatest effect on all water characteristics. Sunlight causes all the changes in water quality. Knowing what it does and how it works is helpful in understanding the relationship of the parameters.

"The sun causes changes in the pH by influencing photosynthesis," explains Cook. "More sun equals more photosynthesis and that means a higher pH. Less sun, of course, means less photosynthesis, more decay and lower pH.

"So the level of sunlight penetration and the amount of it, which depends on the clouds, controls the pH to a good

To professional bass angler Ken Cook, pH readings mean a lot. The former fisheries biologist utilizes the information to help him find more largemouth.

Water Chemistry Factors   245

degree," he continues. "That's why the bass are usually in the weedbeds during the early morning but may not be so concentrated in the afternoon. The pH just becomes too high when the rising sun level causes more photosynthesis."

That's true not only for the "macro-weeds," as Cook calls the large emergent and floating vegetation, but also for the "micro-weeds." The latter are aquatic plant life such as phytoplankton, visible to the naked eye only as green-colored water.

"Phytoplankton are microscopic plants that cause drastic changes in pH by their rapid changes in community levels," says Cook. "They have a very rapid turnover rate and during low light periods, night or cloudy days the lowered photosynthesis rates cause lower pH at the surface.

"That generally means better fishing conditions," he adds. "The decay of phytoplankton is also the reason that pH levels normally decline with depth."

Most fishermen are more productive in shallow water. They are better able to fish the habitat in waters less than 10 feet deep. It's probably easier to establish a shallow pattern through either luck or strategic planning.

Water Clarity Considerations

Clarity of the water affects how the sunlight is able to penetrate depths. It affects how much photosynthesis occurs. It correspondingly affects the biomass of fish that can be supported by a given area of water. Muddy water, for example, cannot produce as many fish because of less sunlight.

"Less sunlight will produce less plankton, and that is the basis of the whole food chain," says Cook. "Turbidity, which reduces sunlight, can be caused by either silt or plankton, however. If the water is brown and muddy, usually you have silt. If it is green water, then usually phytoplankton is abundant.

"Considering the color and clarity of the water is good to a point," he continues, "but too much plankton is a sign of too much fertilization. That could be a result of sewage being pumped into the water you're fishing.

"Areas with plankton that offer less than 12 to 14 inches of visibility are generally poor possibilities for good fishing," explains Cook. "During periods of low light, the oxygen and pH levels just become too low to support fish life."

Water clarity not only affects sunlight penetration and pH, but also oxygen levels. Oxygen is necessary for metabolism but isn't as critical as pH, according to the former biologist. He points out that bass can get plenty of oxygen if the pH is right. But they won't be able to get enough, even in oxygen-rich water, if the pH is outside a range of 7.0 to 9.0.

"The clarity of water also affects bass vision as indicated by Dr. Hill's work with the Color-C-Lector," points out Cook. "My experience indicates that the most visible color should be used predominantly on the lure in either of two situations. The first is very muddy water. The second is in water having low visibility potential due to submerged obstructions, such as weedbeds."

"Otherwise, I like to use a color that is reminiscent of a natural food organism with a splash or flash of the most visible color," he says. "The highly visible color should get the fish's attention, and the lure then should resemble food for a closer inspection. It should imitate preferred forage.

"The clearer the water, the less amount of maximum-visible color should be used," says Cook. "When fishing a crystal clear mountain reservoir, for example, use a jig-and-pig combo that has a base color of black/brown and a flash of the color indicated by the Color-C-Lector."

The opposite would hold true for stained or less-than-clear waters. A lure with the maximum color most visible to bass would draw the most attention and strikes. In other words, the lure coloration should be similar to the color identified by a Color-C-Lector instrument as the best choice.

While some fishing writers don't believe in the Color-C-Lector concept, I totally agree with Cook's conclusions. I have found that indeed the natural coloration of lures was of extreme importance to productivity in very clear waters. The effect of looking exactly like a bass' normal forage diminished as the clarity approached total turbidity. The colors that bass can most readily see then become paramount to attraction.

It makes sense that if the visibility is 20 feet, bass will have ample time to inspect any movement in their environment. They can easily see their forage and any changes in the serenity

The author says locating "invisible" breaklines (pH or water temperatures) will help NAFC members locate the most productive areas to fish.

NAFC Fishing Library

underwater. The probability of them detecting a phony offering is also much higher.

Cook feels the best visibility range for catching bass is 15 to 24 inches. He prefers waters that possess turbidity due primarily to plankton particles, not silt. The bass professional's techniques seem to be most effective in such waters.

"Temperature is often a factor in controlling fish activity and it certainly does to a great degree," notes Cook, "but pH affects the ability of bass to function with temperature. For example, largemouth really don't become active and act like bass until the temperature reaches about 57 degrees if the pH level is outside the preferred range of 7.0 to 9.0. Normal predatory action starts at about 47 degrees if the pH is proper."

The temperature controls not only metabolism of the bass but also that of their food. Thus, in cold water, lures should be retrieved slowly to closely imitate food fish activity. In colder water temperatures the bait selected should be one that does not have an erratic movement. In warmer water you will draw more strikes by using lures with exaggerated, erratic action and by retrieving them faster.

The "Cline" Family And Relations

"Bass especially love border areas," says Cook. "An edge allows predatory fish, such as bass, to do their thing to a high degree of efficiency. This invisible edge can be vertical (shear) or horizontal (cline), and bass and other fish will undoubtedly use it.

"Stratifications normally occur in the summer. Sometimes shallow-water fishing during the dark periods can be very good. Normally in midday you'll need to measure the water quality in relation to depth to determine the presence of clines. Their presence can pinpoint the depth at which to find the most active fish."

A cline is the horizontal breakline where the values of a water quality parameter are very different. Everyone has heard of thermoclines. These are the precise points where water temperature drops quickly in just a couple of feet. It is generally a summer phenomenon, and anglers finding and fishing the top edge of a thermocline usually catch many bass.

Similar clines exist for pH and for clarity, and knowing their location can help a good angler determine the most productive area for bass. According to Cook, pH clines are potentially the most definite parameter in determining the proper depth to fish. That's especially true in the summer when they are most likely to exist. He lists in order of importance the pH cline, the clarity cline and the thermocline.

"The depth of the pH cline normally changes from one area of the lake to another if the clarity changes," says Cook. "That's because of the primary influence of the sun. Muddy water causes shallower clines than clear water because of the effect of the sun's penetration."

Establishing a clarity cline is beneficial because big largemouth often position themselves in the muddier layer for ambushing prey. That cline can most often be found around a runoff due to the different densities of runoff water versus lake water. Often there will be a pH cline in that same area. Cook says these should become primary fishing zones.

No longer is it necessary to use several instruments to measure these factors. The Multi-C-Lector, developed by Joe Meirick and Dick Healey of Lake Systems in conjunction with Dr. Hill, is what Cook employs. The electronic device senses five variables: pH, water clarity, water temperature, probe speed and optimum lure coloration.

"On a typical spring fishing trip, you will find that the pH changes with areas of a lake. You can take the Multi-C-Lector and measure both pH and temperature in the potential areas," advises Cook. "Remember, an area with a good, warm temperature may not be good because of poor pH. Try to find the areas that have both temperature at its maximum and pH at its best—usually highest within the preferred range."

The so-called "invisible" breaklines usually dictate where bass can be found. Today, professional anglers like Ken Cook and weekend fishermen have an opportunity to pinpoint those bass hangouts. To do so no longer requires the interpretative background and sophisticated equipment of a fisheries biologist.

Fish And Game Departments

When you begin to plan your next fishing trip, contact the Fish And Game Department in the state or province you intend to go. They can provide you with valuable information about fishing regulations, non-resident license fees and season dates, as well as answer any specific questions you have.

United States

Alabama Dept. of Conservation &
  Natural Resources
64 N. Union St.
Montgomery, AL 36130
(205) 261-3486

Alaska Dept. of Fish & Game
P.O. Box 3-2000
Juneau, AK 99802
(907) 465-4100

Arizona Game & Fish Dept.
2222 W. Greenway Rd.
Phoenix, AZ 85023
(602) 942-3000

Arkansas Game & Fish Comm.
#2 Natural Resources Dr.
Little Rock, AR 72205
(501) 223-6300

California Dept. of Fish & Game
1416 Ninth St.
P.O. Box 944209
Sacramento, CA 94244
(916) 445-5708

Colorado Div. of Wildlife
6060 Broadway
Denver, CO 80216
(303) 297-1192

Connecticut Dept. of
  Environmental Protection
State Office Bldg.
165 Capital Ave.
Hartford, CT 06106
(203) 566-5599

Delaware Div. of Fish & Wildlife
P.O. Box 1401
Dover, DE 19903
(302) 736-4431

Florida Game & Fresh Water
  Fish Comm.
620 S. Meridan St.
Tallahassee, FL 32399-1600
(904) 488-1960

Georgia State Game & Fish Div.
205 Butler St.
Suite 1362
Atlanta, GA 30334
(404) 656-3523

Hawaii Div. of Aquatic Resources
1151 Punchbowl St.
Honolulu, HI 96813
(808) 548-4000

Idaho Fish & Game Dept.
600 S. Walnut, Box 25
Boise, ID 83707
(208) 334-3700

Illinois Dept. of Conservation
Lincoln Tower Plaza
524 S. Second St.
Springfield, IL 62706
(217) 782-6302

Indiana Div. of Fish & Wildlife
607 State Office Bldg.
Rm. 607
Indianapolis, IN 46204
(317) 232-4080

Iowa Dept. of Natural Resources
Div. of Fish & Wildlife
Wallace State Office Bldg.
E. 9th and Grand Ave.
Des Moines, IA 50319-0034
(515) 281-5918

Kansas Dept. of Wildlife & Parks
RR #2, Box 54-A
Pratt, KS 67124
(316) 672-5911

Kentucky Dept. of Fish &
  Wildlife Resources
#1 Game Farm Rd.
Frankfort, KY 40601
(502) 564-3400

Louisiana Dept. of Wildlife & Fisheries
P.O. Box 98000
Baton Rouge, LA 70898
(504) 765-2800

Maine Dept. of Inland Fisheries & Wildlife
284 State St., Station 41
Augusta, ME 04333
(207) 289-2766

Maryland Dept. of Natural Resources
Tawes State Office Bldg., B-2
Annapolis, MD 21401
(301) 974-3061

Massachusetts Div. of Fisheries & Wildlife
100 Cambridge St.
Boston, MA 02202
(617) 727-3151

Michigan Dept. of Natural Resources
Box 30028
Lansing, MI 48909
(517) 373-1280

Minnesota Dept. of Natural Resources
500 Lafayette Rd.
St. Paul, MN 55155
(612) 296-6157

Mississippi Dept. of Wildlife,
  Fisheries & Parks
P.O. Box 451
Jackson, MS 39205
(601) 961-5300

Missouri Dept. of Conservation
P.O. Box 180
Jefferson City, MO 65102-0180
(314) 751-4115

Montana Dept. of Fish, Wildlife & Parks
1420 E. Sixth St.
Helena, MT 59602
(406) 444-2535

Nebraska Game & Parks Comm.
2200 N. 33rd St.
P.O. Box 30370
Lincoln, NE 68503
(402) 464-0641

Nevada Dept. of Wildlife
P.O. Box 10678
Reno, NV 89520
(702) 784-0500

New Hampshire Fish & Game Dept.
2 Hazen Dr.
Concord, NH 03301
(603) 271-3421

New Jersey Div. of Fish, Game & Wildlife
501 E. State St., CN400
Trenton, NJ 08625
(609) 292-8642

New Mexico Game & Fish Dept.
Villagra Bldg.
Santa Fe, NM 87503
(505) 827-7899

New York Div. of Fish & Wildlife
50 Wolf Rd.
Albany, NY 12233
(518) 457-5690

North Carolina Wildlife
Resources Comm.
Archdale Bldg.
512 N. Salisbury St.
Raleigh, NC 27611
(919) 733-3633

North Dakota State Game & Fish Dept.
100 N. Bismarck Expressway
Bismarck, ND 58501
(701) 221-6300

Ohio Dept. of Natural Resources
Div. of Wildlife
Fountain Square
Columbus, OH 43224
(614) 265-6300

Oklahoma Dept. of Wildlife Conservation
1801 N. Lincoln
P.O. Box 53465
Oklahoma City, OK 73152
(405) 521-3851

Oregon Dept. of Fish & Wildlife
Fish Div.
506 S.W. Mill St.
P.O. Box 59
Portland, OR 97207
(503) 229-5440

Pennsylvania Fish Comm.
P.O. Box 1673
Harrisburg, PA 17105
(717) 657-4518

Rhode Island Dept. of
Environmental Management
Div. of Fish & Wildlife
Oliver Stedman Govt. Center
4808 Tower Hill Rd.
Wakefield, RI 02879
(401) 789-3094

South Carolina Wildlife & Marine
Resources Dept.
Rembert C. Dennis Bldg.
P.O. Box 167
Columbia, SC 29202
(803) 734-3888

South Dakota Dept. of Game,
Fish & Parks
Sigurd Anderson Bldg.
445 E. Capitol
Pierre, SD 57501-3185
(605) 773-3485

Tennessee Wildlife Resource Agency
Div. of Fish Management
Ellington Agricultural Center
P.O. Box 40747
Nashville, TN 37204
(615) 781-6575

Texas Parks & Wildlife Dept.
Fisheries Div.
4200 Smith School Rd.
Austin, TX 78744
(512) 389-4857

Utah State Dept. of Wildlife Resources
1596 W. North Temple
Salt Lake City, UT 84116-3154
(810) 533-9333

Vermont Dept. of Fish & Wildlife
103 S. Main St., 10 South
Waterbury, VT 05676
(802) 244-7331

Virginia Dept. of Game & Inland Fisheries
4010 W. Broad St.
P.O. Box 11104
Richmond, VA 23230
(804) 367-1000

Washington Dept. of Fisheries
115 General Administration Bldg.
Olympia, WA 98504
(206) 753-6600

West Virginia Dept. of Natural Resources
1800 Washington St. E.
Charleston, WV 25305
(304) 348-2754

Wisconsin Dept. of Natural Resources
Bureau of Fish Management
P.O. Box 7921
Madison, WI 53707
(608) 266-7025

Wyoming Game & Fish Dept.
Fish Div.
5400 Bishop Blvd.
Cheyenne, WY 82006
(307) 777-7686

Canada
Alberta Dept. of Forestry, Lands & Wildlife
Fish & Wildlife Div.
Main Floor North Tower
Petroleum Plaza
9945 108th St.
Edmonton, Alberta T5K 2G6
(403) 427-6733

British Columbia Ministry
of the Environment
Recreational Fisheries Branch
Parliament Bldgs.
Victoria, British Columbia V8V 1X5
(604) 387-9710

Manitoba Dept. of Natural Resources
Fisheries Branch
1495 St. James St.
Rm. 101, Box 20
Winnipeg, Manitoba R3H 0W9
(204) 945-6640

New Brunswick Dept. of Natural Resources
Fish & Wildlife Branch
Maritime Forestry Complex
P.O. Box 6000
Fredericton, New Brunswick E3B 5H1
(506) 453-2440

Newfoundland Wildlife Div.
Bldg. 810, Pleasantville
P.O. Box 4750
St. Johns, Newfoundland A1C 5T7
(709) 576-2630

Northwest Territory Dept. of
Renewable Resources
Wildlife Management
Legislative Bldg.
Yellowknife, Northwest Territories X1A 2L9
(403) 873-7760

Nova Scotia Dept. of Land & Forests
Wildlife Div.
Toronto-Dominion Bank Bldg.
1791 Barrington St.
P.O. Box 698
Halifax, Nova Scotia B3J 2T9
(902) 424-5935

Ontario Ministry of Natural Resources
Fisheries Branch
Whitney Block, Queen's Park
Toronto, Ontario M7A 1W3
(416) 965-7885

Prince Edward Island Fish & Wildlife Div.
Dept. of Community Affairs
P.O. Box 2000
Charlottetown, Prince Edward Island
C1A 7N8
(902) 368-4683

Quebec Dept. of Recreation
Fish & Wildlife Div.
Place de la Capitale
150 E., St. Cyrille Blvd.
Quebec City, Quebec G1R 2B2
(418) 643-2207

Saskatchewan Parks, Recreation &
Culture Dept.
Fisheries Branch
3211 Albert St.
Regina, Saskatchewan S4S 5W6
(306) 787-2884

Yukon Dept. of Renewable Resources
Fisheries Management
Box 2703
Whitehorse, Yukon Y1A 2C6
(403) 667-5110

Index

NAFC Fishing Library